Ecclesiastes is not cut from the ... ets settled, and all the answers pr... e-siastes is Reality TV. It's messy ... s blush. I've preached through Ec... sure I got it right. That's why when I ... again I will have Philip Ryken's warm and insigh..., *Why Everything Matters*, at the top of my resource list.

BRYAN LORITTS,
Pastor for Preaching and Mission, Trinity Grace Church,
New York City, New York

The beauty of this book is that it comes from a college president fresh from a decade of ministry in one of America's celebrated pulpits where he preached an extended published series on Ecclesiastes. Here the university audience (with the academic year unfolding) elicits a compactness and piquancy from a godly presidential-fatherly voice. *Why Everything Matters* is a remarkable read that will inform and elevate every heart with essential wisdom for living a life that matters.

R. KENT HUGHES,
Senior Pastor Emeritus, College Church, Wheaton, Illinois
and Visiting Professor of Pastoral Theology,
Westminster Theological Seminary, Philadelphia, Pennsylvania

Why Everything Matters by Philip Ryken is a wonderful treatment of the book of Ecclesiastes. In his study of the text the author beautifully blends the mind of a scholar with the heart of a pastor. It is a faithful exposition of a book that is troubling to many, and I am happy to commend its use to pastors and teachers of God's inspired Word.

DANIEL L. AKIN,
President, Southeastern Baptist Theological Seminary,
Wake Forest, North Carolina

Why Everything Matters will serve you ever so well. It is refreshingly honest. It is consistently insightful (the truths on page 14 and of chapter 8, for example, are worth the price of the book). It is both engaging and culturally engaged (from Herman Melville to Pink Floyd). But ultimately what is most helpful is the fact that this book is marked by the same God-centered, God-focused realism of Ecclesiastes, a thing necessary for those of us who sometimes have to deal with a sense of futility in the midst of the often wearying vexation of daily life. In the end—and all along the way—*Why*

Everything Matters leads us to God, and to finding our joy in him. Whether you are a brand new Christian just beginning to sort through the big questions, or a seasoned believer going over them again, I warmly commend this book to you.

Mike Bullmore,
Senior Pastor, CrossWay Community Church, Bristol, Wisconsin

Some books promise to change your life—President Ryken is more helpful and truthful than that. His wise reading of Ecclesiastes, however, could change the way you navigate the crooked things in life, the way you define success and the way you embrace God's plan amidst this world's injustices.

John Nunes,
Emil and Elfriede Jochum Professor and Chair,
Valparaiso University, Valparaiso, Indiana

We are surrounded every day by people who seek to fill their emptiness with pleasures and achievements. No book in the Bible so clearly addresses this futile search as does Ecclesiastes. And no commentary I've ever read on Ecclesiastes so artfully answers every vain search with the good news of Christ as does Philip Ryken's *Why Everything Matters.*

Andrew Davis,
Senior Pastor, First Baptist Church, Durham, North Carolina

Phil Ryken has made the message of a forgotten book in the Bible clear and applicable to those of us in the 21st Century. Using his literary insights and many contemporary illustrations, he shows us that people in today's world are asking the same questions and that Ecclesiastes points them to the same God who can give us purpose and meaning.

Steven Chin,
Senior Pastor, Boston Chinese Evangelical Church, Boston, Massachusetts

Philip Ryken has provided another crisp, lively and faithful exposition that will serve both Bible reader and Bible teacher alike. This book will be a great help in opening up the wonderful and unique world of Ecclesiastes. Highly recommended.

Sam Allberry,
Associate Minister at St Mary's Church, Maidenhead, UK;
author of *Is God Anti-Gay?* and *James For You.*

WHY EVERYTHING MATTERS

THE GOSPEL IN ECCLESIASTES

PHILIP G. RYKEN

Unless otherwise indicated, Scripture quotations are from *The Holy Bible, English Standard Version* (ESV), copyright © 2001 by Crossway Bibles, a division of Good News Publishers. Used by permission. All rights reserved.

Scripture quotations marked (KJV) are taken from *The King James Version.*

paperback ISBN 978-1-78191-645-2
epub ISBN 978-1-78191-694-0
mobi ISBN 978-1-78191-695-7

Published in 2015
by
Christian Focus Publications Ltd.
Geanies House, Fearn, Ross-shire,
IV20 1TW, Scotland, UK

www.christianfocus.com

Cover design by Daniel van Straaten

Printed by Bell & Bain, Glasgow

CONTENTS

To

the memory of my uncle

– Gerrit Versendaal –

whose life exemplified the virtues that
we read about in Ecclesiastes:

friendship, gratitude, hard work
and joy in the God who gives us every good gift.

PREFACE

Ecclesiastes has something for everyone

The seventeenth-century poet and preacher John Donne discovered that Ecclesiastes spoke to him as a sinful man living in a sinful world. This was partly because the author—who is usually identified as King Solomon—'hides none of his own sins' and 'pours out his own soul in that Book.'[1] By being honest about life's troubles, Ecclesiastes touches the hearts of people who struggle.

Ecclesiastes also has a way of speaking to the issues of the day—any day. When Penn State University was embroiled in a public scandal over the conduct of its football players, former linebacker Matt Millen wanted to put the situation into its biblical context. 'If people out there are thinking that this is new, let me just give you a little bit of Scripture. Ecclesiastes. Nothing is done that hasn't been done before.'[2]

---

1. John Donne, quoted in Christianson, *Ecclesiastes through the Centuries*, 97.
2. Matt Millen, quoted by David Jones and Bob Flounders in 'Lions Were Never All Angels', *The Patriot News* (July 27, 2008).

As much as anything else, Ecclesiastes is for people who have their doubts about God but can't stop thinking about Him. Maybe this explains why Herman Melville—the famous author of *Moby Dick*—returned to Ecclesiastes again and again. One literary critic compared Melville to 'the last guest who cannot leave the party; he was always returning to see if he had left his hat and gloves.'[3] The author of Ecclesiastes had his doubts, too, and these have enabled him to speak to skeptics as well as believers down through the centuries.

One thing that Ecclesiastes doesn't try to do is give us all the answers. Some books are like that: they admit their limitations. Back in the eighteenth century, Dr Samuel Johnson wrote a monumental dictionary. When he was finished with his lexical masterpiece, the prodigious Dr Johnson had a definition for nearly every word in the English language. Yet not for a moment did he think that he knew all the answers. In the preface to his dictionary he echoed Ecclesiastes: 'I saw that one enquiry only gave occasion to another, that book referred to book, that to search was not always to find, and to find was not always to be informed; and that thus to pursue perfection was … to chase the sun.'[4]

Dr Johnson was alluding to Ecclesiastes, whose author found that looking for the meaning of life was like chasing the wind. This desperate image helps us understand Ecclesiastes. Ecclesiastes is not the kind of book that we keep reading until we reach the end and get the answer, like a mystery. Instead, it is a book in which we keep struggling

---

3. James Wood, *The Broken Estate: Essays on Literature and Belief* (New York: Random House, 1999), 29.

4. Samuel Johnson, from the preface to *A Dictionary of the English Language* (London, 1755).

with the problems of life and, as we struggle, we learn to trust God with the questions even when we do *not* have all the answers. This is how the whole Christian life works: it is not just about what we get at the end, but also about the people we become along the way. Discipleship is a journey, not just a destination.

I have read and studied Ecclesiastes many times during my earthly pilgrimage, and each reading has repaid richly my efforts to understand its mysteries. I first learned the book from my father, who has always admired its literary artistry and the many-layered depths of its spiritual meaning. I have taught the book more than once, in the church as well as on the college campus. This time through, I was helped by the wise suggestions that Mary Ryken, Richard Schultz and Dan Treier made for improving what I had written. Readers who want to know more about Ecclesiastes—especially chapters 4 to 5 and 7 to 11, which are only touched on lightly in this little book—might consider consulting the longer commentary that I published with Crossway in 2010.

I hope to return to Ecclesiastes again for as long as I am wrestling with life's many questions and waiting for the day when my long journey ends. Thank you for joining me for part of that journey, as we live for the day when we finally go home to the God who has all the answers.

Philip Ryken
President, Wheaton College, Wheaton, Illinois
February, 2015

1

WHY BOTHER?

Vanity of vanities, says the Preacher,
Vanity of vanities! All is vanity.
What does man gain by all the toil
at which he toils under the sun?

Ecclesiastes 1:2-3

Sociologist Jonathan Kozol met Mrs Washington in the South Bronx, where she and her young son David were living at a homeless hotel close to East Tremont Avenue. The mother and child lived in a first-floor room with three steel locks on the door.

Mrs Washington was dying, and each time Kozol came for a visit, she was visibly weaker. But, oh, the stories she could tell about life on the underside of urban America—stories about poverty and injustice, violence and drugs. Mrs Washington told Kozol about children in her building born with AIDS and about the 12-year-old at the bus stop who was hit by stray gunfire and paralyzed. She told him about the physical abuse she had suffered from Mr Washington and about all the difficulties poor people had getting medical care in the city.

The woman and her son also talked about spiritual things. 'I wonder how powerful God is,' young David admitted in one interview. 'He must be wise and powerful to make the animals and trees and give man organs and a brain to build complex machineries, but He is not powerful enough to stop the evil on the earth, to change the hearts of people.' On a subsequent visit, Kozol looked down at Mrs Washington's bed and saw her Bible open next to her on the quilt. The sociologist asked what part she liked to read. 'Ecclesiastes,' she said. 'If you want to know what's happening these days, it's all right there.'[1]

Why Ecclesiastes?

If Ecclesiastes could help Mrs Washington face her challenges as a single mother living at a homeless hotel in the Bronx, then Ecclesiastes can help anyone living anywhere.

Not everyone would agree with this broad claim. Ecclesiastes takes such a sober view of life that some people doubt the spiritual value of reading it, or even question whether it belongs in the Bible at all. When one of the ancient rabbis read Ecclesiastes, he said, 'O Solomon, where is your wisdom? Not only do your words contradict the words of your father, David; they even contradict themselves.'[2]

Yet I agree with Mrs Washington: if we want to know what is happening these days—if we have trouble understanding

---

1. Jonathan Kozol, *Amazing Grace: The Lives of Children and the Conscience of a Nation* (New York: HarperCollins, 1995), 23, 44.
2. Rabbi Tanhum, Mishnah *Shabbat*, quoted in Tremper Longman III, *The Book of Ecclesiastes*, New International Commentary on the Old Testament (Grand Rapids, MI: Eerdmans, 1998), 27.

why a powerful Creator allows profound evil, or struggle to resolve life's many inconsistencies—it is all right here in this book.

There are many good reasons to study Ecclesiastes. This book *helps us ask the biggest and hardest questions that people still have today*—questions that lie at the heart of life in a fallen world: What is the meaning of life? Why is there so much suffering and injustice? Does God even care? Is life really worth living? The writer asks the tough intellectual and practical questions that people always have, and he is not satisfied with the easy answers that children usually get in Sunday school. In fact, part of his spiritual struggle is with the answers he has always been given. If you are the kind of person who always says, 'Yes, but …', then Ecclesiastes is for you.

Here is another reason to study Ecclesiastes: *it helps us worship the one true God.* For all its doubt and dissatisfaction, this book teaches many great truths about God. It presents Him as the Mighty Creator and Sovereign Lord, the all-powerful ruler of the universe, the only wise God. So reading this book will help us grow in the knowledge of God.

Ecclesiastes will also helps us *live for God and not only ourselves.* The writer had more money, enjoyed more pleasure, and possessed more wisdom than anyone else in the world, yet it all ended in tears. The same thing could happen to us, but it doesn't have to. 'Why make your own mistakes,' the writer constantly is saying to us, 'when you can learn from an expert like me instead?'[3] Then he helps us with everyday issues such as money, sex, power and death, which may be

---

3. This remark comes from Manfred O. Garibotti, who served as a ruling elder of Philadelphia's Tenth Presbyterian Church for more than fifty years.

the most practical issue of all. Old Testament scholar Sandra Richter describes the author of Ecclesiastes as a man who had it all, but discovered that 'having it all' nearly destroyed him. Fortunately for us, when he 'climbs the golden ladder of ultimate success and looks over the brink, he actually has the wherewithal to step back from the edge, climb back down, and tell the rest of us ... that there's nothing up there.'[4]

Ecclesiastes also *helps us to be honest about the troubles of life*. Perhaps this explains why the great American novelist Herman Melville called Ecclesiastes 'the truest of all books'.[5] More than anything else in the Bible, it captures the futility and frustration of a fallen world: the drudgery of work, the emptiness of foolish pleasure and the mind-numbing tedium of everyday life. Think of Ecclesiastes as the only book of the Bible we know was written on a Monday morning, probably by a philosophy major. Reading it helps us to be honest with God about our problems—even those of us who trust in God's goodness. One scholar thus describes Ecclesiastes as 'a kind of back door' that allows believers to have the sad and skeptical thoughts that they would never allow to enter the front door of their faith.[6]

Vanity of Vanities

Ecclesiastes begins with a famous refrain: 'Vanity of vanities, vanity of vanities! All is vanity' (Eccles. 1:2). These are not

4. Sandra Richter, 'Two are Better than One: A Meditation in the Key of We', a devotional shared with the Biblical and Theological Studies Department at Wheaton College in September of 2013.
5. Herman Melville, *Moby Dick* (Boston, MA: C. H. Simonds Co., 1892), 400.
6. Norbert Lohfink, *Qoheleth*, trans. by Sean McEvenue, A Continental Commentary (Minneapolis: Fortress, 2003), 1.

only the first but also nearly the last words of Ecclesiastes (see 12:8). With encapsulating superlatives, the author takes the measure of our existence and declares that it is all meaningless.

But before we go any further, we need to define the word 'vanity'—the 'multipurpose metaphor'[7] that is central to the message of Ecclesiastes. Taken literally, the Hebrew word *hevel* refers to a breath or vapor, like a puff of smoke rising from a campfire or the cloud of steam that comes from a hot breath on a frosty morning. Life is like that: elusive, ephemeral, enigmatic. It disappears as suddenly as it comes. We are here today and gone tomorrow. Thus, the Bible compares our mortal existence to a 'mere breath' (Ps. 39:5), or to 'a mist that appears for a little time and then vanishes' (James 4:14). Breathe in. Now breathe out. Life will pass you by just that quickly—not just today, but all our days, from beginning to end.

So when Ecclesiastes says 'vanity of vanities' it primarily is making a comment on the transience of life. But according to some commentators, the word 'vapor' or 'smoke' also becomes a metaphor for the futility of life itself in this fallen world. The New International Version points in this direction when it offers the following translation: 'Meaningless! Meaningless! ... Utterly meaningless! Everything is meaningless.'

Notice the vast scope of the author's claim: '*everything* is meaningless'; '*all* is vanity' (Eccles. 1:2). Not one single aspect of our existence—and therefore not one single thing that will happen to us today—is free from being frustrated by futility. From the injury at the fitness center to the disharmony in the board room, from the mix-up at the

7. Michael V. Fox, *A Time to Tear Down and a Time to Build Up: A Re-reading of Ecclesiastes* (Grand Rapids, MI: Eerdmans, 1999), 30.

bank to the falling out between close friends, every day we encounter things that seem useless, pointless, even absurd.

To prove his point the author takes the things that people ordinarily use to give meaning or to find satisfaction and then shows how empty they really are. He speaks from experience, because he had tried it all: money, pleasure, knowledge, power—all the things that we try (or are tempted to try) in order to bring satisfaction into our lives.

Some people try to find meaning in what they know, but Ecclesiastes says that 'in much wisdom is much vexation, and he who increases knowledge increases sorrow' (Eccles. 1:18). This is hardly something that any self-respecting college would say in its promotional materials for prospective students: 'Come increase your knowledge and add to your sorrows!' But honestly, aren't there some things you wish that you *didn't* know about life?

Some people try to find satisfaction in all the pleasures that money can buy. The author of Ecclesiastes was rich enough to conduct a thorough experiment, but in the end he concluded that there was 'nothing to be gained under the sun' (Eccles. 2:11). So, he threw himself into his work, trying to do something significant. But this also proved to be vexation, because he failed to get a good return on his investment. I wonder: when you come to the end of your life, or even to the end of this year, what will you have to show for all your hard work?

Not even the life of the mind could save this man's desperate soul. Later in the book he will give us the testimony of a frustrated philosopher: 'When I applied my heart to know wisdom, and to see the business that is done on earth, how neither day nor night do one's eyes see sleep, then I saw all the work of God, that man cannot find out the work that is done under the sun. However much man may toil in seeking, he will not find it out. Even though a wise man claims to know, he cannot find it out' (Eccles. 8:16-17). 'Of making many books there is no end,' he will go on to say in the final chapter, 'and much study is a weariness of the flesh' (Eccles. 12:12). If we doubt the truth of this statement, all we need to do is ask the nearest scholar and he will tell us the truth: Vanity of vanities, vanity of vanities! All is vanity.

Same Old, Same Old

We begin to get a good sense of Ecclesiastes and its attitude about life from the question posed at the beginning of the book and the poem that is offered by way of an answer. Here is the question:

> *What does man gain by all the toil*
> *at which he toils under the sun?*

Then comes the answer:

> *A generation goes, and a generation comes,*
> *but the earth remains forever.*
> *The sun rises, and the sun goes down,*
> *and hastens to the place where it rises.*
> *The wind blows to the south*
> *and goes around to the north;*
> *around and around goes the wind,*
> *and on its circuits the wind returns.*
> *All streams run to the sea,*
> *but the sea is not full;*
> *to the place where the streams flow,*
> *there they flow again.*
> *All things are full of weariness;*
> *a man cannot utter it;*

the eye is not satisfied with seeing,
nor the ear filled with hearing.
What has been is what will be,
and what has been done is what will be done,
and there is nothing new under the sun.
Is there a thing of which it is said,
'See, this is new?'
It has been already
in the ages before us.
There is no remembrance of former things,
nor will there be any remembrance
of later things yet to be
among those who come after (Eccles. 1:3-11).

A good title for this poem would be 'Same Old, Same Old'. The writer is making his case for the weary emptiness of our tired existence and wondering why he should bother. In verses 4 through 7 he looks at the elemental things of nature—earth, air, fire and water—and sees no real change anywhere. Generations come and go, but the earth does not move. With weary monotony the sun rises and sets, rises and sets, rises and sets. The wind goes around and around in circles. The water flows forever into the sea. It is all the same as it ever was.

I witness the same boring cycle on the campus of Wheaton College. August rolls around and we're back in chapel for another Academic Convocation. It may be new for freshmen, but it is not new in itself. Some faculty members start a new year at Wheaton thirty or forty times in the course of their careers, and as a college we have held an opening chapel service for more than 150 years. There is nothing new under the sun. It's just the same old, same old. As they say in France, 'Plus ça change, plus c'est la même chose.'[8] The author of Ecclesiastes gets tired just thinking about all of this. The *Contemporary English Version* translates verse 8 like this: 'All of life is far more boring than words could ever say'.

So, why bother? That *is* the question. Why keep running on 'the treadmill of our existence'?[9] In verses 8 to 11, the writer moves from the natural world to human experience and sees the same thing that he saw in nature: things are done over and over again without any real profit or genuine progress. If the sun, the wind, and the mighty rivers have nothing to show for their constant motion, then what hope do we have of ever accomplishing anything in life? Pink Floyd seems almost to offer a paraphrase of Ecclesiastes in a song from *The Dark Side of the Moon*:

> *So you run and you run to catch up with the sun but it's sinking*
> *Racing around to come up behind you again.*
> *The sun is the same in a relative way but you're older,*
> *Shorter of breath and one day closer to death.*[10]

The spirit of Ecclesiastes 1 is captured equally well in a short poem by Stephen Crane:

> *I saw a man pursuing the horizon;*
> *Round and round they sped.*
> *I was disturbed at this;*
> *I accosted the man.*

---

8. Or as we would say it in English, 'The more things change, the more things stay the same.'
9. Derek Kidner, *The Message of Ecclesiastes*, The Bible Speaks Today (Downers Grove, IL: InterVarsity, 1976), 15.
10. Roger Waters, 'Time', *The Dark Side of the Moon* (Harvest, 1973).

'It is futile,' I said,
'You can never—'
'You lie,' he cried,
And ran on.[11]

Some people try to escape life's monotony and futility by filling their senses with what they see and hear. Today, we see an endless procession of visual images (YouTube, Instagram, Netflix) and listen to an endless stream of sounds (Pandora, Grooveshark), but we are never satisfied. There is always one more show to watch, one more game to play, one more song to listen to. What Ecclesiastes says is still true: 'The eye is not satisfied with seeing, nor the ear filled with hearing' (Eccles. 1:8). We're insatiable in appetite. Even if we have seen before, we want to see more. But what do we really gain? What progress do we make in life, spiritually or otherwise?

We experience the same thing on the larger scale of human events: 'What has been is what will be, and what has been done is what will be done, and there is nothing new under the sun' (Eccles. 1:9). How is *that* for a philosophy of history—humanity on a hamster wheel? Future generations will suffer the same plight. As Philip Larkin wrote in one of his bleak poems:

Man hands on misery to man.
It deepens like a coastal shelf.
Get out as early as you can,
And don't have any kids yourself.[12]

---

11. Stephen Crane, *The Black Riders and Other Lines* (Boston: Copeland and Day, 1896), 25.
12. Philip Larkin, *The Complete Poems*, ed. by Archie Burnett (Farrar, Straus and Giroux, 2013), as quoted in Thom Satterlee, 'Larkin's Monument', *Books and Culture* (July/August 2013), 37.

The writer of Ecclesiastes makes such sweeping claims about future futility that we are tempted to try and think of a counter-example. Surely there must be at least one thing that is new under the sun. For a moment, the writer considers that possibility and asks, 'Is there a thing of which it is said, "See, this is new"?' But just as quickly, he denies it. Whatever *seems* new 'has been already in the ages before us' (Eccles. 1:10).

By way of example, consider the so-called discovery of the New World. 'In 1492, Columbus sailed the ocean blue', right? Yet Columbus was hardly the first European to set foot on North America. In those days, Basque fishermen were already crossing the Atlantic to fish for cod off the coast of Newfoundland. Not that they told anyone about it, of course, because who would ever reveal a secret fishing spot? The merchants of Bristol, England, were more vocal. They wrote Columbus after his triumphant return to complain that he knew perfectly well *they* had been to America before him.[13] This is to say nothing of Leif Ericson and the Norse explorers who reached the New World five hundred years before!

The more things change, the more they stay the same. And if it ever seems like there really *is* something new under the sun, it is only because we have forgotten what happened before—the way people will forget about us one day, when there is nothing left of us except a faded picture in a discarded scrapbook, or perhaps a digital image in a forgotten corner of cyberspace.

All Things New

'Vanity of vanities! All is vanity!' So, why bother? This is the question that Ecclesiastes throws in our faces. But if we

13. See Mark Kurlansky, *Cod: A Biography of the Fish That Changed the World* (New York: Penguin, 1998).

find ourselves starting to agree with its philosophy, then it is crucially important to understand the book's purpose. 'The function of Ecclesiastes,' writes Derek Kidner, 'is to bring us to the point where we begin to fear that such a comment (all is vanity) is the only honest one' and then have to 'face the appalling inference that nothing has meaning, nothing matters.'[14] But this is not the only honest view of life. It is only the way things appear *if* we merely look at them 'under the sun'.

This phrase, which occurs in verses 3 and 9 of chapter 1 and dozens of other places in Ecclesiastes, is one of the keys to understanding the book. 'Under the sun' expresses the extent of our problem. Where do we experience life's futility and frustration? Everywhere the sun shines.

Yet this phrase also opens up the possibility of a different perspective. To see things 'under the sun' is to look at them from the ground level, taking an earthly point of view and leaving God out of the picture. If that is all we do, then we are bound to reach the same conclusion as the novelist Henry Miller: 'Life has to be given a meaning because of the obvious fact that it has no meaning.'[15] But of course this is not the right way to look at anything. There is a God who rules *over* the sun. So we are not limited to the terrestrial; we can also get outside our own solar system and see things from a celestial perspective.

Ecclesiastes begs us to do that. It shows us the weariness of our existence so that we will not expect to find meaning and satisfaction in earthly things, but only in God above. Money, sex, power, achievement—none of these things

---

14. Kidner, *Message of Ecclesiastes*, 20.

15. Henry Miller, 'Creative Death,' *The Wisdom of the Heart* (New York: New Directions, 1941), 5.

satisfy—only God does. This does not mean, of course, that if we believe in God we stop feeling the vanity of life under the sun. We *do* feel it. But Ecclesiastes shows our need for an 'above the sun' perspective that brings joy and meaning to life. According to Augustine, the author wrote the book in order to suggest 'with such fullness as he judged adequate, the emptiness of this life, with the ultimate objective, to be sure, of making us yearn for another kind of life which is no unsubstantial shadow under the sun but substantial reality under the sun's Creator.'[16]

One way to gain this divine perspective is to take all of the things that make life so wearisome and see what a difference it makes when we bring God back into the picture. Ecclesiastes looks at the natural world and fails to see any progress. But the psalmist looks at the same old sun and says it 'comes out like a bridegroom leaving his chamber, and, like a strong man, runs its course with joy' (Ps. 19:5). Whether the sun makes any progress or not, it bears witness to the joy and strength of its Creator. Therefore, 'From the rising of the sun unto the going down of the same the LORD's name is to be praised' (Ps. 113:3 KJV).

The very repetition we see in nature is a testimony to the goodness of God, showing the constancy of our Creator. The winds blow at His bidding and the waters flow at His command, blessing every creature. Scripture says that God 'lays the beams of his chambers on the waters; he makes the clouds his chariot; he rides on the wings of the wind' (Ps. 104:3). 'He draws up the drops of water; they distill his mist in rain, which the skies pour down and drop on

---

16. Augustine, 'City of God', 20.3, in *Proverbs, Ecclesiastes, Song of Solomon*, ed. by J. Robert Wright, Ancient Christian Commentary on Scripture, OT 9 (Downers Grove, IL: InterVarsity, 2005), 261.

mankind abundantly' (Job 36:27-28). Rather than seeing the day-in, day-out routine the way Ecclesiastes sees it, we can give the same testimony as the great African American scientist George Washington Carver: 'I love to think of nature as unlimited broadcasting stations, through which God speaks to us every day, every hour, and every moment of our lives, if we will only tune in and remain so.'[17]

Looking above the sun also gives us a different perspective on human experience. Is anything new? Maybe not under the sun, but the God who rules over the sun is always doing something new, especially in Jesus Christ, who is the exception that proves the rule.[18] God has made a *new covenant* for us in the blood of Jesus Christ (Luke 22:20)—the blood He shed on the cross for the forgiveness of all our sins. If we ask the question, 'Why bother?' the answer is that we have a Savior who looked at all the futility and frustration we suffer in this fallen world and chose to suffer it with us and for us so that He could actually do something about it.

Then there is the *new life* that came up from the empty tomb when Jesus rose from the dead with the power of eternal salvation. There is the *new heart* that God gives to everyone who believes in Jesus (Ezek. 36:26). There is the *new creation* that comes when the Holy Spirit enters our minds and hearts (2 Cor. 5:17). Once we give our lives to Jesus Christ it is never the same old, same old ever again. The living God sits on the throne of the universe and says, 'Behold, I am making all things new' (Rev. 21:5).

---

17. George Washington Carver, in William Federer, *George Washington Carver: His Life and Faith in His Own Words* (St Louis, MO: Amerisearch, 2002), 71-73.

18. Daniel J. Treier, *Proverbs & Ecclesiastes*, Brazos Theological Commentary on the Bible (Grand Rapids, MI: Brazos, 2011), 129.

One day, this great God will make a new heaven and a new earth. Life's frustrations will not last forever; we live in the hope of a new day, when the vaporous mist of this life will vanish and eternity will dawn in the brightness of our Savior's glory. In one of the earliest commentaries ever composed on Ecclesiastes, Didymus the Blind wrote these illuminating words: 'A person who is enlightened by the "sun of righteousness" is not "under" it but "in" it. Thus it is said in the Gospel: "The righteous will shine like the sun in the kingdom of their Father", not "under" the sun.'[19]

Almost every verse in Ecclesiastes shows us how much we need a Savior to make all things new. When John Wesley preached his way through this great book of the Bible, he described in his journal what it was like to begin his sermon series. 'Began expounding the Book of Ecclesiastes,' he wrote. 'Never before had I so clear a sight either of its meaning or beauties. Neither did I imagine, that the several parts of it were in so exquisite a manner connected together, all tending to prove the grand truth, that there is no happiness out of God.'[20]

Remember this whenever you get frustrated, sad, angry or disappointed with everything in life that is getting broken, falling apart, and going wrong. Remember this when you feel overwhelmed and are tempted to wonder why you should even bother—with your work, with a relationship, with your faith. You were made for a new and better world. The very

---

19. Didymus the Blind, *Commentary on Ecclesiastes* 46.7 in *Ancient Christian Commentary on Scripture* IX ed. by J. Robert Wright (Downers Grove, IL: InterVarsity Press, 2005), 213.

20. From the entry to John Wesley's journal for January 2, 1777, as quoted in R. N. Whybray, *Ecclesiastes*, New Century Bible Commentary (Grand Rapids, MI: Eerdmans, 1989), xii-xiii.

fact that you are weary of this life is pointing you to Jesus as the only One who can satisfy your soul.

2

THE ULTIMATE QUEST

I the Preacher have been king over Israel in Jerusalem.
And I applied my heart to seek and to search out by
wisdom all that is done under heaven.

ECCLESIASTES 1:12-13

In *The Hitchhiker's Guide to the Galaxy* Douglas Adams writes about Deep Thought, the powerful supercomputer tasked with determining 'the Answer to Life, the Universe, and Everything'. It takes the computer a long time to check and double check its computations—seven and a half million years, to be exact—but eventually it spits out a simple, unambiguous answer: the meaning of life is 42.

'Forty-two!' someone yells at the computer. 'Is that all you've got to show for seven and a half million years' work?'

'I checked it very thoroughly,' Deep Thought replies, 'and that quite definitely is the answer. I think the problem, to be quite honest with you, is that you've never actually known what the question is.'[1]

---

1. Douglas Adams, *The Hitchhiker's Guide to the Galaxy* (London: Pan Books, 1979), 162.

Deep down, everyone wants to know the meaning of life, but to get the right answer we have to ask the right question in the right way. This is our quest in Ecclesiastes: to come to a true, accurate understanding of life, the universe and everything—which hopefully will take less than seven and a half million years!

Authorship

Our guide on this journey is called Qoheleth, or as we know him in English, 'the Preacher'. Before we go any further it is important to clarify this man's identity. The Hebrew root of the word *qoheleth* literally means 'to gather or assemble'. Some scholars take this as a reference to the way the author collected wise sayings. But in the Old Testament the verbal form of this word typically refers to gathering a community of people, especially for the worship of God. So think of Qoheleth as a preacher or teacher speaking wisdom to the people of God.

This context is reflected in the book's English title. 'Ecclesiastes' comes from Greek, not Hebrew. It is a form of the word *ekklesia*, which is the common New Testament word for 'church'. Taken most literally, Ecclesiastes means 'one who speaks to the congregation'[2]—in a word, the 'Preacher'. This Preacher is further identified as 'the son of David, king in Jerusalem' (Eccles. 1:1). Naturally, we think first of King Solomon, the only immediate son of David to rule in Jerusalem after his father. Besides, many of the things that Qoheleth tells us about his life experience sound like Solomon. Who else could say, 'I have acquired great wisdom, surpassing all who were over Jerusalem before me' (Eccles. 1:16)?

As the author describes the houses he built, the gardens he planted and the women he kept, we are reminded repeatedly

2. Whybray, *Ecclesiastes*, 2.

of the power and luxury of King Solomon. Then, at the end of the book, the author is described as 'weighing and studying and arranging many proverbs with great care' (Eccles. 12:9), which also sounds a lot like Solomon. The name Qoheleth fits, too, because when Solomon dedicated the temple in Jerusalem, he gathered his people and led them in the worship of God. In describing that great assembly, the Bible repeatedly uses the same root word that Ecclesiastes uses for the name of its author, *qoheleth* (see 1 Kings 8:1).

So, the church has long identified Solomon as the Preacher of Ecclesiastes. According to this point of view, after wandering away from God and falling into tragic sin, that wise king repented of his wicked ways and turned back to God. Ecclesiastes is his memoir, or last testament, in which he tells us what he learned from his hopeless attempt to live without God.

More recently, some scholars have moved away from identifying Solomon as the book's author. They point out that he is never mentioned by name (the way he is in Proverbs, for example). If Solomon wrote this book, then why doesn't he come right out and say so?[3] Although the opening verse associates the book with that famous king, it never explicitly identifies him as the author. Furthermore, the Preacher says things that some people find it hard to imagine Solomon ever saying, such as when he starts to criticize wealthy kings for oppressing the poor (e.g. Eccles. 5:8).

Thus, some scholars believe that Ecclesiastes was written after the time of Solomon, possibly during Israel's exile in Babylon or even later. They point out that in ancient times it was conventional to write fictional autobiographies, in which a writer would take on the persona of someone famous—not to deceive anyone, but to deliver a message.

3. Fox, *A Time to Tear Down and a Time to Build Up*, 159.

Perhaps Ecclesiastes is the same kind of book—a fictional royal autobiography, in which a second 'Solomon' uses the life of Israel's famous king to illustrate his philosophy of life. Who better to show the emptiness of life without God than the wisest, richest man who ever lived? In effect, the author gives us a literary argument from the greater to the lesser. He slips on the sandals (so to speak) of a man who had everything that anyone could ever want. But the world is not enough. If it could not satisfy Solomon, it will never satisfy anyone.

All things considered I tend to agree with the conclusion of Richard Schultz, who encourages us to read Ecclesiastes from a Solomonic perspective, accepting the possibility if not the necessity that Solomon wrote the book himself.[4]

The Seeker's Quest

After introducing the author (Eccles. 1:1) and stating the theme (Eccles 1:2), Ecclesiastes offers a series of examples (Eccles. 1:3-11) taken from nature and from human experience to prove that the world is 'endlessly busy and hopelessly inconclusive.'[5] These verses come from someone who refers to the Preacher in the third person—perhaps the book's final editor.

Then, starting in verse 12, Qoheleth speaks for himself and invites us on a spiritual and intellectual quest: 'I the Preacher have been king over Israel in Jerusalem. And I applied my heart to seek and to search out by wisdom all that is done under heaven' (Eccles. 1:12-13). Ecclesiastes is a 'thinking

---

4. Richard L. Schultz, 'Ecclesiastes', in *The Baker Illustrated Bible Commentary*, ed. by Gary M. Burge and Andrew E. Hill (Grand Rapids, MI: Eerdmans, 2012), 581.

5. Kidner, *Message of Ecclesiastes*, 28.

person's book.'[6] Its author was a seeker who always asked the ultimate questions. Here he writes from the vantage point of age and experience, telling us what he learned from his lifelong quest to understand the meaning of life.

This description of interests and passions fits what we know about King Solomon. When David's son became king, God gave him the opportunity of a lifetime: he could ask for anything he wished. Wisely, Solomon chose wisdom. God was so pleased with this request that he said, 'Behold, I give you a wise and discerning mind, so that none like you has been before you and none like you shall arise after you' (1 Kings 3:12). But this precious gift did not mean that the king instantly understood everything. He still had to apply himself to the pursuit of knowledge, which is exactly what he did.

Solomon's quest was *sincere*. He devoted his heart and soul to knowing the truth. His quest was *comprehensive*. The words 'seek' and 'search' in verse 13 show how serious he was.[7] Solomon wanted to take it all in, leaving nothing out, so that his conclusions about life would be as definitive as possible. He wanted to investigate every area of human endeavor—'all that is done under heaven' (Eccles. 1:13). This quest was also *commendable*. Rather than seeking pleasure, or looking for popularity, or finding significance in personal accomplishments, the Preacher pursued the life of the mind. Solomon was the kind of person who, given the choice, would attend a liberal arts college and major in philosophy.

---

6. Walter C. Kaiser, *Coping with Change—Ecclesiastes* (Fearn, Ross-Shire: Christian Focus, 2013), 12.

7. As Dan Treier points out, these words also tie in with the life of Solomon: in 1 Kings 3:9, 12 and 2 Chronicles 1:10, 12, Solomon receives a 'heart' and 'wisdom' from God (Treier, *Proverbs & Ecclesiastes*, 135).

Understand that the kind of wisdom he pursued was not divine, but human—the best that human beings have thought or said. Here 'wisdom' refers to what people can learn about the world without special revelation from God. This is a worthy pursuit, as far as it goes. All truth is God's truth, wherever it may be found. Because God created the world, and everything in it, any truth that we discover is a divine gift; 'the LORD gives wisdom; from his mouth come knowledge and understanding' (Prov. 2:6). But the question still needs to be asked: how far will human wisdom take us? Will information bring transformation? Can it lead us to everlasting life?

A Bad Business

One way to answer these questions is to see the result of Qoheleth's quest. What did he discover? The reality is that he came up empty. Rather than totaling 42, the meaning of life did not add up for him at all.

Verses 13 to 15 summarize the author's unhappy efforts to understand the universe. His mood is unmistakably gloomy: 'It is an unhappy business that God has given to the children of man to be busy with' (Eccles. 1:13). Sooner or later, most people end up feeling the same way. Many things in life make us feel unhappy: the bad relationship our parents have, the unkind comments people make about us, the things we do not have but wish we did, the recognition we deserve but never get—even the ordinary frustrations of daily life can make us feel unhappy.

When the Preacher talks about 'unhappy business' (or 'evil business'), he may be referring to the things that people do—human activity. If so, then what he says is certainly true. Ever since the sin of our first parents, work has been cursed. Leonard Woolf, the publisher and political theorist who co-founded the Bloomsbury Group (also the husband of Virginia Woolf), had this to say about his life's work:

> I see clearly that I have achieved practically nothing. The world today and the history of the human anthill during the past five to seven years would be exactly the same as it is if I had played Ping-Pong instead of sitting on committees and writing books and memoranda. I have therefore to make a rather ignominious confession that I must have, in a long life, ground through between 150,000 and 200,000 hours of perfectly useless work.[8]

Leonard Woolf wrote more than twenty books on literature, politics and economics. Yet in the end it all seemed like a complete waste of time. As we think about all our own hard work it is tempting to feel the same way: life is a bad business.

There is another way to take this verse, however. The 'unhappy business' that Qoheleth has in mind may be his very quest to understand the meaning of life.[9] The pursuit of knowledge *itself* is what turns out to be such a bad business. The longer he looked for answers and the harder he tried to understand the meaning of life, the more frustrated he became with all of life's unanswerable questions and impenetrable enigmas.

It is worth considering how we feel about our efforts to understand life. Sooner or later, most people who wrestle with the big questions end up getting discouraged or depressed. This is normal. It happened, for example, to the first president of Wheaton College, Jonathan Blanchard. Blanchard later became a national leader in the fight against slavery. But as a

---

8. Leonard Woolf, quoted in *Wireless Age* (September/November, 1998).

9. Whybray, *Ecclesiastes*, 49.

student at a Christian liberal arts college, he suffered a season of spiritual depression. In other words, Blanchard had failed to heed the sound advice of the Renaissance scientist Francis Bacon not to 'submit the mysteries of God to our reason.'[10] Eventually, he understood why: in searching for the meaning of life, he had 'acquired the habit of looking at truths with a kind of philosophic curiosity rather than a reasonable humility.'[11]

The quest for knowledge is one of our God-given tasks. As people made in the image of God we cannot help but ask the ultimate questions. Even people who deny God's existence keep searching for the meaning of their existence. Consider what the irreverent comedian Louis C.K. said in a television interview. Louis C.K. was talking about why he hates cell phones, and he was trying to be funny, but in fact he was baring his soul:

> Underneath everything in your life there's that thing—that 'empty', forever empty. ... Just that knowledge that it's all for nothing and you're alone. You know, it's down there. And sometimes, when things clear away—you're not watching anything, you're in your car, and you start going, 'Oh, no, here it comes! That I'm alone.' You know, it starts to visit on you—just this sadness. Life is tremendously sad, just by being in it.[12]

---

10. Francis Bacon, quoted in Charles Bridges, *A Commentary on Ecclesiastes* (1860; repr. Edinburgh: Banner of Trusth, 1961), 207.
11. Clyde S. Kilby, *Minority of One: The Biography of Jonathan Blanchard* (Grand Rapids, MI: Eerdmans, 1959), 32.
12. Louis C.K., as interviewed on *Conan*, September 20, 2013 (http://www.youtube.com/watch?v=5HbYScItf1c&feature=youtu.be&desktop_uri=%2Fwatch%3Fv%3D5HbYScItf1c%26feature%3Dyoutu.be&app=desktop).

Striving after the Wind

Qoheleth experienced the same emptiness. After going everywhere and looking at everything he reached the following conclusion: 'I have seen everything that is done under the sun, and behold, all is vanity and a striving after wind' (Eccles. 1:14).

Again we hear some of the Preacher's favorite phrases. He is looking 'under the sun', seeing what people do from an earthly perspective. He repeats the word 'vanity', or 'vapor'. Then he introduces another metaphor that encapsulates his philosophy of life. Life under the sun is 'a striving after wind'. There is some uncertainty about the best way to translate the word 'striving' (Hebrew *re'ut*). It can mean 'chasing', or something more like 'shepherding'. But neither of these activities has any hope of catching the wind!

The same is true of all our human efforts to understand our existence. From what the Preacher had seen, based on personal experience, figuring out the meaning of life was like trying to hold the wind in your hands. Many intelligent minds have reached the same conclusion, such as the infamous atheist Richard Dawkins, who stated that human existence is 'neither good nor evil, neither kind nor cruel, but simply callous: indifferent to all suffering, lacking all purpose.'[13] Or consider Louis C.K.'s answer to the meaning of human existence: 'You just feel kind of satisfied with your products, and then you die.'[14]

The Preacher-King concluded the first stage of his unhappy quest with a proverb: 'What is crooked cannot be made straight, and what is lacking cannot be counted' (Eccles. 1:15). Some things in life are crooked—not in the sense that they are criminal or immoral, but in the sense

---

13. Richard Dawkins, *River out of Eden* (New York: Basic Books, 1995).

14. Louis C.K. *op. cit.*

that they are so bent out of shape that they resist all our efforts to make them straight. There are many things in life that we wish we could fix, but can't, any more than we can repair a crumpled fender using our bare hands. We suffer longstanding family conflicts, estrangement between former friends, wrongs done to us by someone in power, disease or disability, our own moral failings, the accidents we caused—the list goes on and on. There is always something in life we wish we could bend back into shape. And sometimes our efforts to do so actually end up making things worse.

Alas, Qoheleth too had learned that 'what is crooked cannot be made straight.' No matter how hard we try, we cannot bend our lives in a different direction. There are people we cannot manage, problems we cannot solve, pressures we cannot escape.

Nor can we make life add up, which is the point of the second line in this proverb. The *Good News Bible* translates verse 15 like this: 'You can't straighten out what is crooked; you can't count things that aren't there.' The Turkish novelist Orhan Pamuk said something similar: 'unfinished, the world is somehow lacking.'[15]

Life is like an account that refuses to balance. We can tell that there is a deficit, but we can't figure out exactly what it is. And even when we make an adjustment to get everything to add up correctly, deep down we know that somehow we are fudging the figures.

The Quest Continued

So, Qoheleth's first quest failed. Human wisdom could not provide an answer for the meaning of life. This does not

15. Orhan Pamuk, *Other Colors: Essays and a Story*, as quoted in Colin Thubron, 'Locked in the Writer's Room', *The New York Review of Books* (November 8, 2007), 54.18.4.

mean that he was ready to give up, however. In verses 16 to 18 he continues his quest. After his first attempt ended in failure, he had a heart-to-heart talk with himself, a running internal dialogue about what he had discovered. He said to his soul, 'I have acquired great wisdom, surpassing all who were over Jerusalem before me, and my heart has had great experience of wisdom and knowledge' (Eccles. 1:16).

Still, the Solomon of Ecclesiastes had not yet considered the claims of morality, so his quest was incomplete. He had tried to learn everything he could, like someone who goes to a liberal arts college and reads all the great books. But he had not yet fully investigated the difference between right and wrong, or tried to find meaning and purpose by becoming a better person. So he took a comparative approach: 'I applied my heart to know wisdom and to know madness and folly' (Eccles. 1:17).

Here the Preacher seems to use 'madness and folly' the way they are usually used in the Old Testament: to refer to the crazy foolishness of disobedience to God. He was trying to understand the difference between right and wrong, which is an approach that many people take today. Even if they are not sure where God fits in, or whether there is a god at all, they still want to lead good, moral lives. Like the character that Bill Murray portrays in the movie *Groundhog Day*, they try to make the best of life's monotony by doing good to other people.

What was the result of Qoheleth's renewed quest? Did knowing the difference between right and wrong help him find purpose in life? Was he able to become a better person? Not at all. Conventional morality also failed to satisfy his soul. He said, 'I perceived that this also is but a striving after wind' (Eccles. 1:17). Then he offered another proverb to encapsulate what he had discovered: 'For in much wisdom is much vexation, and he who increases knowledge increases sorrow' (Eccles. 1:18). This is why people say that ignorance is bliss: the more we know about life, the more sorrows we have.

A Hopeful Conclusion

As usual, reading Ecclesiastes quickly makes us feel even worse about life than we did before. At first the Preacher's honesty may seem refreshing, but the more we study his book, the more depressed we become.

This actually means that the writer is achieving his purpose. Remember that he is showing us the world from a merely earthly perspective—the best thinking that human beings can do on their own.[16] Qoheleth believes in God, of course, and mentions Him by name (see verse 13), but he made his spiritual quest essentially without God's help. The Preacher did not pray or consult Scripture. Instead, he was off and running on his own quest for meaning without stopping to consider the majesty of God. He was probing 'into the depth of matters by his unaided and unenlightened reason apart from any disclosures of truth that God has granted.'[17]

If we take a secular perspective and try to understand the world on our own terms rather than on God's terms, we will never escape Ecclesiastes 1. Study all the philosophy, research all the religion and pursue all the personal improvement that you please—it will still end in frustration. Human reason can only take us so far. All our learning is empty without God.

Thank God that there is a God, and that He does not leave us in despair! The Solomon of Ecclesiastes shows us the

16. Kidner, *Message of Ecclesiastes*, 31.

17. H. C. Leupold, *Exposition of Ecclesiastes* (Grand Rapids, MI: Baker, 1952), 55.

Savior we need. Qoheleth didn't know it yet, but at the end of all our questing God will be waiting for us in the Person of His own Son. The Bible says that God rewards people who truly seek Him (Heb. 11:6), and that if we lack wisdom, we should ask God and He will give it to us (James 1:5). Jesus Christ—He Himself, in His own person—is 'the wisdom of God' (1 Cor. 1:24).

We should not leave Ecclesiastes 1 without remembering that Jesus entered into all the vanity and vexation of life under the sun to show us the wise way to live. If we follow Jesus and His wisdom we will not try to bend what is crooked back to our own purpose, but humbly submit to the way God wants things to be, just as Jesus did when He went to the crooked cross and died for our sins (see 1 Pet. 2:21-24).

If we follow the wisdom of Jesus Christ eventually life will add up. It will never add up to something as simple as 42, of course, and it may not ever seem to add up on this side of eternity. But leave the final calculations to Jesus, and He will make sure that all the books balance in the end, including our personal account, which He has reconciled with His own blood.

Our present vexation will not last forever, including all our struggles to understand the meaning of life. Soon, our sorrows will be over. We will be with Jesus forever, and find the answers to all our questions in Him.

3

MEANINGFUL HEDONISM

I said in my heart, 'Come now, I will test you with pleasure; enjoy yourself.' But behold, this also was vanity.

ECCLESIASTES 2:1

Most Americans today experience more pleasure than most people in the history of the world. Yet in spite of our prosperity—or maybe because of it—we still suffer from poverty of soul. The taste of pleasure has grown our appetite for this world beyond satisfaction. Meanwhile, we are still searching desperately for meaning in life.

Peggy Lee talked about this problem in the song, 'Is That All There Is?' In the second stanza, she describes her childhood experience of going to the circus:

> When I was 12 years old, my father took me to a circus, the greatest show on earth. There were clowns and elephants and dancing bears, and a beautiful lady in pink tights flew high above our heads. And so I sat there watching the marvelous spectacle. I had the feeling that something was

> missing. I didn't know what, but when it was over, I said to myself, 'Is that all there is to a circus?'

Then Peggy Lee croons her famous refrain: 'Is that all there is? Is that all there is? If that's all there is, my friends, then let's keep dancing. Let's break out the booze and have a ball, if that's all there is.'[1]

The Pleasure Test

The Solomon of Ecclesiastes had the same question as Peggy Lee: Is that all there is to life, or is there something more? First he tried to think his way to an answer, using his mind to figure out the mysteries of existence. But his quest for knowledge through human intellect ended in vexation and sorrow. 'Autonomous epistemology', he discovered, is vanity.[2]

So, the Preacher decided to take another approach. He started talking to himself again—not about something life-changing like the grace and beauty of God, but about getting more out of life. He said to his soul: 'Come now, I will test you with pleasure; enjoy yourself' (Eccles. 2:1).

The word 'test' indicates that what follows is an experiment, a deliberate attempt to learn something from personal experience. The word 'pleasure' shows what he wants to experience: the good life. He is like 'The Wanderer' in the song U2 wrote for Johnny Cash: 'I went out there / In search of experience / To taste and to touch and to feel as much / As a man can before he repents.'[3]

---

1. 'Is That All There is?' by Jerry Leiber and Mike Stoller, as recorded in *Peggy Lee's Greatest Hits, Volume 1* (Curb Records).
2. Craig G. Bartholomew, *Ecclesiastes*, Baker Commentary on the Old Testament Wisdom and Psalms (Grand Rapids, MI: Baker, 2009), 135.
3. U2, 'The Wanderer', as sung with Johnny Cash on *Zooropa* (Island Records, 1993).

Another important word which gets repeated in every single verse in this passage is the word 'I'. Admittedly, the writer is speaking autobiographically. But does he need to say 'me, myself, and I' quite so often (almost 40 times in these verses)? Clearly he is self-indulgent in the pursuit of self-centered pleasure.

And so Qoheleth became an experimental hedonist, choosing to make his own personal happiness his main purpose in life. In a perverse reversal of the first answer in the *Westminster Shorter Catechism*, his chief end was to glorify *himself* and enjoy *himself* as much as he could. This is a temptation for all of us: to please ourselves rather than to please God. To avoid this error, it is good for us to ask ourselves this question: What pleasures am I tempted to take for myself instead of seeking the pleasure of God?

Let the Good Times Roll

Almost immediately the Preacher tells us that this new quest failed as spectacularly as the first one did. Pleasure did not satisfy his soul any more than wisdom. 'Behold,' he says, 'this also was vanity' (Eccles. 2:1). Although it seemed to hold out the promise of purpose, pleasure vanished like the mist, leaving the Preacher with nothing. The pursuit of pleasure turned out to be meaningless hedonism.

Lest we think that the Preacher failed to give hedonism a fair chance, in verses 2 through 8 he lists all of the pleasures he tried, followed in verses 9 to 11 by a personal reflection on what he learned from his experience.

First he experimented with comedy. Some people deal with their insecurities by joking about something. When they get down on themselves, they make fun of other people. When they are bored, they look for something to give them a giggle, such as a funny clip on YouTube—anything to get a laugh.

The Preacher tried this sort of thing too, yet it failed to bring him lasting fulfillment. 'I said of laughter, "It is mad," and of pleasure, "What use is it?"' (Eccles. 2:2). Here 'madness' indicates 'moral perversity rather than mental oddity.'[4] There is a kind of joyful laughter that brings glory to God. But some joking is superficial, or else cynical. If we are wise, we will ask whether our laughter comes from rejoicing in the goodness of God or comes at someone else's expense.

Qoheleth discovered that when it comes to the meaning of our existence, laughter is a useless pleasure. Life is hardly a laughing matter, and there is certainly nothing funny about the funeral of someone who dies without Jesus Christ.

The next pleasure Qoheleth tried was alcohol, which is another popular way to seek enjoyment in life—or else to escape its troubles. Knowing this, the Preacher-King chose to 'cheer his body with wine' (Eccles. 2:3). Maybe this means that he was abusing alcohol the way many people do today—not receiving wine as a gift from God, but drinking to get drunk.

Yet Qoheleth claimed that his heart was still guiding him with wisdom. In one of his famous proverbs, Solomon said, 'Wine is a mocker, strong drink a brawler, and whoever is led astray by it is not wise' (Prov. 20:1). But maybe Qoheleth's wine-tasting was a controlled experiment. Like the ancient Epicureans, he was drinking in moderation and then soberly assessing his experience. Maybe he was not an alcoholic after all, but a connoisseur.

Either way—whether his wine-drinking was marked by sophistication or inebriation—the man was looking for pleasure while he still had the time. The end of verse 3

4. Kidner, *Message of Ecclesiastes*, 31.

introduces a prominent theme in the rest of the book: namely, the brevity of life. Because life is so short, we need to pursue pleasure while we still can. This sentiment has never been expressed more clearly or memorably than in a popular beer commercial from the 1960s and 70s: 'You only go around once in life: Go for all the gusto you can!'

The Finer Things in Life

The Solomon of Ecclesiastes grabbed for all of that gusto, but he still came up empty. There are many other pleasures in life, and the Preacher-King was rich enough to try almost all of them. He built a beautiful home, where he planted magnificent gardens: 'I made great works. I built houses and planted vineyards for myself. I made myself gardens and parks, and planted in them all kinds of fruit trees. I made myself pools from which to water the forest of growing trees' (Eccles. 2:4-6).

Qoheleth was an architect, a builder and a developer. Once again, we are reminded of King Solomon. Whether Ecclesiastes was written by Solomon himself or by someone who presented that famous king's tragedy as a cautionary tale, the details in this chapter come from his biography. Solomon spent more than a decade building a magnificent palace. He was skilled in viniculture, the production of wine. He was equally involved in horticulture and silviculture, planting flowers and fruit trees. This lush vegetation was irrigated by reservoirs large enough to water a small forest.

Only a great man could even attempt such a grand project. The scope of his achievement is indicated by the fact that Qoheleth mentions everything in the plural: houses and vineyards, gardens and parks, trees and pools. Best of all, it was all for him. These 'great works', as the Bible calls them, were part of the man's private residence. The palace of the Preacher-King was paradise regained—a man-made Garden of Eden.

Given the vast scope of his building projects and the huge size of his property, the Preacher-King needed a massive work force. To that end he purchased many slaves, and to feed them all, many flocks and herds ranged across his royal ranch (Eccles. 2:7). We see all of this in the life of King Solomon, who had countless servants waiting on him hand and foot (see 1 Kings 10:4-8), and so many animals that every day the chefs in his royal kitchen prepared 'ten fat oxen, and twenty pasture-fed cattle, a hundred sheep, besides deer, gazelles, roebucks, and fattened fowl' (1 Kings 4:23).

Needless to say, the Preacher-King also had a lot of money—some from taxing his own people, and some from foreign tribute: 'silver and gold and the treasure of kings and provinces' (Eccles. 2:8; cf. 1 Kings 10:14-29). He used some of this money to make beautiful music, both literally and figuratively: 'I got singers, both men and women, and many concubines, the delight of the sons of man' (Eccles. 2:8).

Music was a rare pleasure in those days, but the man who wrote Ecclesiastes could afford to bring it into his own home, where choirs sang at his pleasure. Sex is more common, but few people have ever experienced it on the scale of King Solomon, who had a thousand sexual partners in his royal harem (1 Kings 11:3).

Here is how the Preacher-King summarized his experiment with pleasure: 'So I became great and surpassed all who were before me in Jerusalem. . . . And whatever my eyes desired I did not keep from them. I kept my heart from no pleasure' (Eccles. 2:9-10). Rather than waiting for God to make him great, as God had promised (1 Kings 1:37), the Solomon of Ecclesiastes made himself great. Whenever he saw something he wanted, he took it. Whenever he was tempted to indulge in a fleshly pleasure, he gave in. He denied himself nothing—nothing 'visibly entertaining or inwardly satisfying.'[5]

Foolish Pleasure

Wine, women and song: the Solomon of Ecclesiastes had it all. Today his face would be on the cover of *Fortune* magazine, his home featured in a photo spread with *Architectural Digest*. Pop stars would sing at his birthday party; supermodels would flirt for his affections.

It is hard not to envy the man, at least a little bit. Wouldn't *you* like to live like a king (or a queen)? Don't you wish that you had someone to do your dirty work for you? Honestly, if you could get away with it, wouldn't you grab some of Solomon's gusto for yourself?

Before you say 'yes', you need to know the result of his experiment. What happens to people who pursue any and every pleasure as their main passion in life?

Many of us know the answer already. We have as many opportunities as Solomon had to indulge in sinful and selfish desires. In fact, maybe he would envy us. Generally speaking, we live in better homes, with better furniture and climate control. We dine at a larger buffet and listen to a much wider variety of music. As far as sex is concerned, we can download an endless parade of virtual partners—a harem for the imagination. Everything is offered to us. Nothing is unavailable. So let me ask: are we satisfied, or do we still want more?

---

5. Michael A. Eaton, *Ecclesiastes: An Introduction and Commentary*, Tyndale Old Testament Commentaries (Downers Grove, IL: InterVarsity, 1983), 67.

We are not satisfied, of course. As David Hubbard wisely observes, pleasure's advertising agency is much more effective than its manufacturing department![6]

Or consider what Gregg Easterbrook says in his book *The Progress Paradox*, which is subtitled *How Life Gets Better While People Feel Worse*. Easterbrook shows that we have more of almost everything today ... except happiness. In fact, the more we have, the unhappier we become, because we know that we will never be able to get all the new things that we want.[7] Maybe this helps to explain why the twenty-first century is an age of anxiety, when more people struggle more with mental illness than ever before.

Then again, maybe none of this is new. When Alexis de Tocqueville toured the United States in the 1830s he noticed the 'strange melancholy' that haunted Americans 'in the midst of abundance'. The French statesman wisely concluded that 'the complete joys of this world will never satisfy the heart'.[8]

On 'the morning after', while he was still suffering the after-effects of his pleasure trip, Qoheleth said: 'Then I considered all that my hands had done and the toil I had expended in doing it, and behold, all was vanity and a striving after wind, and there was nothing to be gained under the sun' (Eccles. 2:11).

The verb 'consider' (Hebrew *panah*) literally means 'to face', to look something right in the eye. Solomon was facing up to reality, looking at life the way it really is, and he wants

---

6. David A. Hubbard, *Ecclesiastes and Song of Songs*, Mastering the Old Testament (Dallas, TX: Word, 1991), 35.

7. Gregg Easterbrook, *The Progress Paradox: How Life Gets Better While People Feel Worse* (New York: Random House, 2003), 124.

8. Timothy Keller, *Counterfeit Gods: The Empty Promises of Money, Sex, and Power, and the Only Hope That Matters* (New York: Dutton, 2009), x.

us to know that it isn't pretty. Squeeze all the pleasure out of life that you can, and still there is nothing to be gained from living under the sun. Pleasure, pursued for its own sake, cannot satisfy our souls.

We will either learn this lesson from Ecclesiastes, or else we will learn it from our own melancholy experience. Just ask Tom Brady, the star quarterback of football's New England Patriots, who wanted to know, 'Why do I have three Super Bowl rings and still think there's something greater out there for me? I mean, maybe a lot of people would say, "Hey man, this is what is." I reached my goal, my dream, my life. Me, I think, "It's got to be more than this." I mean this isn't, this can't be what it's all cracked up to be.' When the interviewer asked, 'What's the answer?' Brady could only say, 'I wish I knew. I wish I knew.'[9]

Longing for God

If we don't know the answer, then maybe all we can do is cue Peggy Lee again: 'If that's all there is, my friends, then let's keep dancing. Let's break out the booze and have a ball, if that's all there is.'

But that is *not* all there is—praise God! When finally we discover that all the pleasures we pursue under the sun cannot satisfy our souls, then maybe we will look beyond this world. Our unsatisfied longings are a spiritual clue that we were made to enjoy the pleasures of God. This world leaves us with what social critic Andrew Delbanco has described as an 'unslaked craving for transcendence'.[10] This is by design. If

9. See interview at http://www.cbsnews.com/stories/2005/11/03/60minutes/main1008148_page3.2html.

10. Andrew Delbanco, *The Real American Dream*, quoted in Easterbrook, 248.

we were able to find lasting satisfaction in earthly pleasure then we would never see our need for God. But satisfaction does not come in the pleasures themselves; it is always sold separately.

Our dissatisfaction should point us back to God—not away from Him, but toward Him. In fact, C. S. Lewis claimed that in the disappointment of our unmet desire, we live 'a sort of ontological proof' for the existence of God.[11] Maybe this is why Ecclesiastes is in the Bible. It is here to convince us that satisfaction only comes in God Himself. The world is not enough. Ecclesiastes does not show us this to make us discouraged or depressed, but to drive us back to God. This is *not* all there is. We were made for another world. There is a God in heaven, who sent His Son to save us and then to satisfy us.

In order to accomplish this saving purpose God's great Son could not live to please Himself, but had to live for His Father's pleasure. Think of it like this: 'Everything Solomon pursued, Jesus was tempted by, but resisted.'[12] This makes Him the Savior that every dissatisfied sinner needs, the man that Johnny Cash was looking for in 'The Wanderer': 'one good man / A spirit who would not bend or break / who could sit at his Father's right hand.'[13]

Meaningful Hedonism

We are offered total satisfaction in the crucified and risen Christ. To quote a line from the colonial poet Anne

---

11. C. S. Lewis, *The Pilgrim's Regress: An Allegorical Apologetic for Christianity, Reason, and Romanticism*, 3rd edn. (Grand Rapids, MI: Eerdmans, 1958), 10.

12. Mark Driscoll, 'Setting the Record Crooked', *Preaching Today* (Issue 266).

13. 'The Wanderer' (1993).

Bradstreet, only Jesus 'satiates the soul'.[14] When we turn to Him, something surprising happens: the very pleasures that failed to satisfy us now help us to find even greater joy in the goodness of God. This is not true of foolish pleasures, of course—what the Bible calls 'the fleeting pleasures of sin' (Heb. 11:25). But there is such a thing as holy pleasure. For the people of God there is *meaningful* hedonism: pleasure that comes in the presence of Jesus Christ.

Late in the fantasy *Prince Caspian*, from the Narnia Chronicles, C. S. Lewis portrays the sisters Lucy and Susan having 'a romp' with Aslan. The great lion-king has returned to the Land of Narnia and awakened the forest. There is raucous dancing, with laughter and shouting, and a feast of luscious grapes that taste like wine. A wild boy is dancing there, 'dressed only in a faun-skin, with vine-leaves wreathed in his curly hair'. Lucy and Susan's brother Edmund looks at the boy and remarks, 'There's a chap who might do anything—absolutely anything.'

Later, the children figure out that the wild youth was Bacchus, also known as Dionysius—the god of wine. This prompts Susan to make a wise observation: 'I wouldn't have felt very safe with Bacchus and all his wild girls if we'd met them without Aslan.' 'I should think not,' Lucy replies.[15]

The principle applies well to the Christian life: pleasure is only safe for us when God is there. This never happens when we take pleasure for ourselves, or make it our main passion in life. It only happens when we receive every pleasure as

---

14. Anne Bradstreet, 'The Vanity of All Worldly Things', in *Chapters into Verse: Poetry in English Inspired by the Bible*, 2 vols, ed. by Robert Atwan and Laurence Wieder (New York: Oxford University Press, 1993), 1:354.

15. C. S. Lewis, *Prince Caspian* (New York: MacMillan, 1951), 139.

a gift from God, the way David did when he said, 'In your presence there is fullness of joy; at your right hand are pleasures forevermore.' (Ps. 16:11).

We taste God's pleasure when we receive laughter as a gift from Him—not mocking other people or joking in a vulgar way, but laughing at ourselves and our limitations, knowing that one day we will enter our Master's joy (see Matt. 25:21).

We taste true pleasure when we receive wine as a gift from God, drinking it 'with a merry heart' (Eccles. 9:7)—not tasting it unlawfully or making a mockery of ourselves by getting intoxicated.

We taste God's pleasure when we design good homes and other beautiful buildings, provided that we build them for the good of other people and the glory of God (e.g. Neh. 12:27-30), not for our own grandeur.

We taste God's pleasure when we stroll through a beautiful garden, feast our eyes on the colors of creation, and see the beauty of God.

There is pleasure in everything that Solomon mentions: in rewarding work that is done for the glory of God (Col. 3:23), in feasting at a banquet table with thanksgiving (1 Tim. 4:3-4), in silver and gold that is invested in the kingdom of God, with the guarantee of an eternal return (see Matt. 6:19-21). There is pleasure in music that delights the ear and moves our emotions to the worship of God.

There is pleasure in sexual relations when they are shared as the Designer intended. When sexual intimacy is given to someone else rather than taken for ourselves, and when it is shared exclusively between one man and one woman who are bound by a love covenant for life, then intercourse finds its highest pleasure.

God is not a spoilsport. He is not trying to take any pleasure away from us, but to give us more. Once we learn how to find our satisfaction in God Himself, then all His gifts become the best and truest pleasures. As Daniel Treier has written, 'the divine gifts of creation are meant to be enjoyed as matters of stewardship rather than possession.'[16] Happily, we do not have to be as rich as Solomon to experience meaningful hedonism. We simply have to receive what is in the world around us as a gift from a loving God, and then give thanks to Him in the name of Jesus Christ.

---

16. Treier, *Proverbs & Ecclesiastes*, 136.

4

WORKING THINGS OUT

What has a man from all the toil and striving of heart with which he toils beneath the sun? For all his days are full of sorrow, and his work is a vexation. Even in the night his heart does not rest. This also is vanity.

Ecclesiastes 2:22-23

If you're like most people, you reach a point every week when you wonder how you can possibly get everything done. You're behind in your work, a major assignment is due, you have important commitments to keep and there just don't seem to be enough hours in the day.

If this describes your life then perhaps you can relate to something that the poet Christian Wiman wrote in one of his essays: 'Ask anyone how they're doing these days, and the most frequent response will be some form of "busy" or "tired". We all feel that there is somehow less time than there once was' to satisfy 'the feverish need we have to fill every hour of every day with measurable tasks and accomplishments.'[1]

1. Christian Wiman, *Ambition and Survival: Becoming a Poet* (Port Townsend, WA: Copper Canyon Press, 2007), 116.

The lack of time to get everything done explains why I have long been an advocate of 'Grunsday'—an extra day every week between Wednesday and Thursday, just for catching up on the stuff that we can't seem to get done the rest of the week.

Then there is all the frustration we experience in the work that we *do* manage to get done. Most working people can relate to the opening lines of 'Five O'Clock World', by The Vogues:

> Up every morning just to keep a job
> I gotta fight my way through the hustlin' mob
> Sounds of the city poundin' in my brain
> While another day goes down the drain.[2]

Another day working is another day wasted. The Solomon who wrote Ecclesiastes felt the same way. Maybe he never had to pull an 'all-nighter' at school or commute to his job every day in heavy traffic, but like the rest of us the Preacher-King suffered the curse of work.

You Can't Take It With You

Remember Qoheleth's quest. In headlong pursuit of the meaning of life, the author of Ecclesiastes (either Solomon or his ghostwriter) indulged in all the pleasures of the flesh (and I do mean 'all'). Afterwards he reconsidered the advantages of wisdom, as compared to folly. But no matter what he tried, his quest failed. Eventually he ended up hating everything under the sun, and one of the things he hated the most was work: 'I hated all my toil in which I toil under the sun' (Eccles. 2:18).

Many people expect work to give them a sense of purpose in life. Perhaps this explains why one of the first things

---

2. Allen Reynolds, 'Five O'Clock World' (1965).

people ask when they meet someone new is 'What do you do for a living?' But work is the wrong place to look for meaning in life.

According to Ecclesiastes—which in many ways is a 'working person's book'[3] as well as a 'thinking person's book'—there are two main problems with our earthly business. The first is that in the end someone else will profit from all our hard work. As a bottom-line thinker, the Preacher wanted to know what kind of return he would get on his investment. As he thought about death (see Eccles. 2:16), he realized that one day he would have to leave everything behind for 'the man who will come after' (Eccles. 2:18).

You can spend your whole life gathering a collection, or building a business, or making a home, or amassing a fortune—but you can't take it with you. Maybe you will lose it when you die, or maybe the loss will happen sooner, through some misfortune. But either way, eventually your collection will go to a dealer, the contents of your home will be sold at auction, someone else will manage your portfolio, and everything you have worked a lifetime to gain will be gone.

If you're lucky your possessions will end up in good hands. Then again, maybe they won't. The Preacher says, 'Who knows whether he will be wise or a fool? Yet he will be master of all for which I toiled and used my wisdom under the sun. This also is vanity' (Eccles. 2:19). We can never be totally sure what will happen after we die, but the question 'Who knows?' invites a negative response. With so many fools in the world, chances are that everything will fall into the wrong hands.

Besides, even if the person who gets our property is wise, he won't deserve it. What we gain from our toil ought to belong to

3. Kaiser, *Coping with Change – Ecclesiastes*, 12.

us, as the reward for all our labor. Instead, it will go to someone else. In light of this sad reality, the Preacher considered the worst-case scenario: 'I turned about and gave my heart up to despair over all the toil of my labors under the sun, because sometimes a person who has toiled with wisdom and knowledge and skill must leave everything to be enjoyed by someone who did not toil for it. This also is [*if Qoheleth said it once, he said it a thousand times*] vanity and a great evil' (Eccles. 2:20-21).

One person does the work, but another person gets the wealth. It's just not fair! Rather than working for our own profit, we end up working for the slacker who gets our stuff when we die. Solomon felt this loss keenly. When he talked about someone working 'with wisdom and skill', he was thinking of all the buildings he built and gardens he planted, not to mention his massive fortune (see Eccles. 2:4-9). Solomon was the world's most successful businessman. But when the king died, he left all of his earnings as a bequest for his oldest son, Rehoboam. King Solomon may not have known whether his successor would be wise, but *we* certainly do: Rehoboam was such a fool that he lost more than eighty percent of his father's kingdom (see 1 Kings 12)!

This is one of the great frustrations of human existence. We are born with a deep longing to have something, make something or do something that will last. Yet the under-the-sun reality is that we will spend our whole lives working to gain something we can never keep. Doubtless this explains why the comedian Woody Allen quipped, 'I don't want to achieve immortality through my work. I want to achieve it by not dying.'[4] The great Russian novelist Leo Tolstoy wrote in a more serious vein:

4. Woody Allen, quoted in Steven Pinker, 'The Brain: The Mystery of Consciousness', *Time* (January 19, 2007), 70.

> My question—that which at the age of fifty brought me to the verge of suicide—was the simplest of questions, lying in the soul of every man … a question without an answer to which one cannot live. It was: 'What will come of what I am doing today or tomorrow? What will come of my whole life? Why should I live, why wish for anything, or do anything?' It can also be expressed thus: Is there any meaning in my life that the inevitable death awaiting me does not destroy?[5]

The Curse of Work

Leaving it all behind is bad enough, but there is another serious problem with work, and that is the work itself! The first problem is that our work will be someone else's reward. The second problem is that our work itself is toil and trouble: 'What has a man from all the toil and striving of heart with which he toils beneath the sun? For all his days are full of sorrow, and his work is a vexation. Even in the night his heart does not rest. This also is [*here it comes again*] vanity' (Eccles. 2:22-23).

When the Preacher talks about toiling 'beneath the sun', we imagine someone working long, hot hours out in the fields, sweating under the burning heat. But work also makes its mental demands, which is why he calls it 'striving of heart'. No matter what kind of work we do it always takes its toll on us. In the words of one paraphrase, there is 'too much strain, without much gain.'[6]

Then think of all the worry that work brings. Sometimes we have so much work to do that we worry about getting it

---

5. Leo Tolstoy, *A Confession*, quoted in Timothy Keller, *The Reason for God: Belief in an Age of Skepticism* (New York: Dutton, 2008), 201.

6. James Limburg, *Encountering Ecclesiastes: A Book for Our Time* (Grand Rapids, MI: Eerdmans), 33.

all done. It would help if we could get a full night's sleep; instead, we lie awake at night obsessing about how we did on yesterday's test or worrying about tomorrow's project.

There is no rest for the weary. Notice how long our problems will last: all our days, according to verse 23. From beginning to end, life is a weary labor, with nothing to show for it. If we make our work our life, it will leave us empty.

Warren Schmidt learned this lesson in the 2002 film *About Schmidt*. After retirement, as Schmidt looks back on his life as an actuary for an Omaha insurance company, he realizes that he has little or nothing to show for all his weary labors. Here is what he writes to the child he has started to sponsor in Africa:

> I know we're all pretty small in the big scheme of things, and I suppose the most you can hope for is to make some kind of difference. But what kind of difference have I made? What in the world is better because of me? ... Once I am dead and everyone who knew me dies too, it will be as though I never even existed. What difference has my life made to anyone? None that I can think of. None at all. Hope things are fine with you. Yours truly, Warren Schmidt.[7]

It's a question for all of us to consider: What kind of difference will I make with my life? Will I have anything to show for all my hard work? King Solomon gave the same answer as Warren Schmidt. When he considered what he gained from his labor under the sun, he concluded that 'all his days are full of sorrow' (Eccles. 2:23).

---

7. Warren Schmidt, played by Jack Nicholson, in *About Schmidt* (New Line, 2002).

Take This Job and Love It!

Nothing prepares us for what comes next, because suddenly Ecclesiastes takes a surprising turn. Without any warning the Preacher says the first truly positive thing in the entire book. Up until this point he has sounded like a workaholic who hates his work and has nothing to show for it. We might even be tempted to agree with the erudite Old Testament scholar Gerhard von Rad in characterizing Qoheleth as a bitter skeptic 'suspended over the abyss of despair'.[8] But suddenly he says, 'There is nothing better for a person than that he should eat and drink and find enjoyment in his toil. This also, I saw, is from the hand of God, for apart from him who can eat or who can have enjoyment?' (Eccles. 2:24-25).

These verses are an oasis of optimism in a wilderness of despair. Thus they mark a turning point in Ecclesiastes—not just on the subject of work, but for the entire argument of the book. Martin Luther called the end of Ecclesiastes 2 'a remarkable passage, one that explains everything preceding and following it.' It is 'the principal conclusion,' Luther said, 'in fact the point, of the whole book.'[9]

Not everyone would agree. Some scholars think that the perspective on life in these verses is still fairly negative. The words 'there is nothing better', they say, express only a grudging appreciation of the good things in life. The author 'couches his language in a way that communicates his reluctance and lack of enthusiasm'.[10] as if to say, 'It isn't much, but at least life can offer you this.' If this interpretation is correct, then the attitude of the Preacher is *carpe diem*, or

8. Gerhard von Rad, quoted in Whybray, *Ecclesiastes*, 12.

9. Martin Luther, 'Notes on Ecclesiastes', in *Luther's Works*, trans. and ed. by Jaroslav Pelikan, 56 vols. (St Louis, MO: Concordia, 1972), 15:46.

10. Longman III, *Book of Ecclesiastes*, 107.

'seize the day', as it says in Corinthians: 'Let us eat and drink, for tomorrow we die' (1 Cor. 15:32).

Yet I believe that Ecclesiastes 2:24-26 is more positive. Indeed, it is the first of the book's 'enjoyment passages'. The Preacher is not giving in to despair here but beginning to see the difference it makes to live with God at the center. He is not seizing something for himself but receiving it from God. Thus, his message is not simply vanity under the sun but also joy from the hand of God. In the words of one commentator, 'It is important not to make one of these claims the only message of the book and dismiss the other as either a distraction or a grudging qualification. Qoheleth insists on both, and often in the same passage.'[11]

Qoheleth's paradox calls to mind an old cartoon in which a publisher is pleading with a novelist to change his opening line: 'Mr Dickens, either it was the best of times or it was the worst of times. It can't be both.'[12] But of course it *can* be both, and often is. There is a bittersweet balance. We live in a world that is cursed by sin, but it is also a world that God created good, that He has visited in the flesh and that He is working to redeem through a cross-bearing crucifixion and a life-giving resurrection. Thus, we experience both the agony and the ecstasy.

Notice carefully what brings the joy. In verse 24 the Preacher embraces some of the very activities that he has already rejected for their failure to bring meaning to life.

---

11. Elizabeth Huwiler, 'Ecclesiastes', in Roland Murphy and Elizabeth Huwiler, *Proverbs, Ecclesiastes, Song of Songs*, New International Biblical Commentary, Old Testament (Peabody, MA: Hendrickson, 1999), 12:165.

12. The *New Yorker* cartoon is quoted in Robert K. Johnston, *Useless Beauty: Ecclesiastes through the Lens of Contemporary Film* (Grand Rapids, MI: Baker, 2004), 169.

Earlier he concluded that work was a total drag. Not even the pleasures of food and drink could satisfy his soul. But now he eats and drinks and finds enjoyment in his toil.

What makes the difference? God makes the difference! Up to this point in Ecclesiastes God has hardly been mentioned, and when He has, He has seemed to be part of the problem. Indeed, this was one of the Preacher's greatest struggles. Inevitably God seemed to be responsible for his troubles. Qoheleth never gave up his faith in the power and sovereignty of God, but rather than making him feel better about things, the truth of God's existence sometimes made him feel worse. If our frustrations with life are also frustrations with the God who gave it to us in the first place, then what hope do we have that life will ever make sense?

But here God's presence makes all the difference. No one can ever find any true joy in anything apart from Him. So, if we are having trouble finding enjoyment in life, God must not be at the center of things for us. If we are deeply dissatisfied, this could be the reason: we have been taking good things and making them ultimate things, when in fact they are God-given things.[13]

By contrast, the eating and drinking that the Preacher enjoys in verse 24 come directly 'from the hand of God'. Qoheleth has stopped trying to seize pleasure for himself and has started to savor it as a gracious gift (see also Ecclesiastes 3:13). Here is a basic biblical principle that we can apply to many situations in life: 'Everything created by God is good, and nothing is to be rejected *if* it is received with thanksgiving, for it is made holy by the word of God and prayer' (1 Tim. 4:4-5, emphasis added).

---

13. Keller, *Reason for God*, 162.

Earthly pleasures are a gift from God. They have their limits, of course, so they will never give us eternal satisfaction. But the joy they bring encourages us in the worship of God. 'Isn't it strange,' asks Ray Stedman, 'that the more you run after life, panting after every pleasure, the less you find, but the more you take life as a gift from God's hand, responding in thankful gratitude for the delight of the moment, the more that seems to come to you.'[14] It is strange, but true: when we receive the good things in life as a gift rather than taking them as an entitlement, we experience genuine joy and true thanksgiving. 'So, whether you eat or drink,' the Scripture says, 'or whatever you do, do all to the glory of God' (1 Cor. 10:31).

Even work is a gift from God when we receive it from His hand. This has been true since the very beginning. Sometimes we imagine that Adam and Eve had nothing to do in the Garden of Eden, when in fact God gave them good hard work to do (Gen. 1:28; 2:15). Unfortunately, because of Adam's sin our work has been cursed, which turns our labor into toil and trouble. But there is still a basic goodness about work that comes from our Creator. We were made in the image of a working God, and when we work for Him we feel His pleasure (see Eccles. 2:10).

For the believer in Christ, our true Boss and ultimate Master is the Savior who gave His life for our sins. Whatever our job happens to be—whether we work as a teacher or a student, an office worker or a construction worker, in food service or financial services, we are working for Christ and for His kingdom. To say this another way, adopted from one of Qoheleth's recurrent images, we are working under the

14. Ray Stedman, *Is This All There Is to Life?* (Palo Alto, CA: Discovery House, 1999), 651-54.

Son, and not simply under the sun: 'Whatever you do, work heartily, as for the Lord and not for men, knowing that from the Lord you will receive the inheritance as your reward. You are serving the Lord Christ' (Col. 3:23-24).

The Fruit of Our Labor

The inheritance of a reward takes us back to an issue we considered previously: What does the worker gain for all his toil? The Preacher had started to wonder whether he would ever get anything at all under the sun. But when he brought God back into the picture, he found this reward: 'For to the one who pleases him God has given wisdom and knowledge and joy, but to the sinner he has given the business of gathering and collecting, only to give to one who pleases God. This also is vanity and a striving after wind' (Eccles. 2:26).

Here the Preacher makes a clear distinction between two kinds of people: those who are under the favor of a gracious God and those who are lost in their sins. Notice how the people who please God are described. They are the grateful recipients of wisdom and knowledge and joy. If we live for God's pleasure, we will be richly rewarded with all of the spiritual blessings that God loves to give.

For the impenitent sinner there is no reward, only loss. It is the sinner, especially, who finds work to be a total frustration. He refuses to receive the blessings of life as gifts from God. His only business is 'gathering and collecting'. In other words, his life is dominated by the acquisition and accumulation of consumer goods. But eventually he will have to leave it all behind and this, indeed, is vanity.

Sometimes the transfer of property takes place already in the present life. During World War I, when my grandfather was growing up in central Iowa, local Dutch farmers were the victims of persecution. Their language sounded like German to some Americans who resented their work ethic, their prosperity and perhaps even their strong commitment to Christ. Dutch farms were vandalized; their produce was burned and their lives were threatened.

The FBI sent men to investigate. They cracked the case wide open when one of the ringleaders boasted about his plans to a secret agent at a local saloon. Not only were the criminals arrested, but eventually many of them were forced into foreclosure. Their farms were snatched up at bargain prices by local Dutch farmers (!), and thus the Scripture was fulfilled: the sinners gathered and collected, only to give what they had to people whose work was pleasing to God.

This doesn't always happen, of course. In fact, one of the vanities of a fallen world is that the righteous often suffer affliction, while many sinners seem to prosper. But it will not always be like this. At the end of history, the meek really will inherit the earth, just as Jesus promised (Matt. 5:5).

In the meantime, we have the reward of our work—not just the fruit of our labor, but the labor itself. God has given us good work to do. We do this good work knowing that Jesus has already done the hard work of our salvation. Jesus Christ was a working man (see John 4:34, 5:17), and seeing Him from this perspective can have a transformational effect on the attitude we have about our own work. Think especially of all the heavy lifting that Jesus did on the cross, where He carried the full weight of our sin all the way to the death—what theologians call 'the finished work of Christ'.

Jesus is still working today through the ministry of His church (see John 9:4; Acts 1:1; Eph. 4:12). We share in this good work by singing God's praise, loving our neighbors, giving people the gospel and praying for God's kingdom to come. We also share in this good work by doing ordinary daily tasks in a way that gives glory to God. It is all kingdom work. As Martin Luther once said, 'the entire world [should] be full of service to God, not only the churches but also the home, the kitchen, the cellar, the workshop and the field.'[15] We can add the classroom, the studio, the laboratory and the cubicle to Luther's list—or whatever favorite spot we have for reading a book or writing on a laptop.

Are you finding God's strength in the work that He has given you to do? Thomas Hughes captures the joy of kingdom work in his novel *Tom Brown's Schooldays*. One of Tom's classmates at boarding school is George Arthur, a frail boy who contracts a life-threatening fever. Arthur has never been strong enough to run and climb and play and fight like other boys. During his illness, he fears that he will never be able to work like other men. Yet one night he has a dream that fills his heart with joy—a vision of the redemption of work:

> And on the other bank of the great river I saw men and women and children; the tears were wiped from their faces; they put on glory and strength; and all weariness and pain fell away. And they worked at some great work. They *all* worked. Each worked in a different way, but all at the same work. And I saw myself, Tom; and even *I* was working and singing.[16]

Whatever you are involved in right now, and whatever you are planning to do with the rest of your life, are you busy with the great work of Jesus Christ? Each of us works in a

---

15. Martin Luther, from his sermon on Matthew 6:24-34, as quoted in Ewald M. Plass, *What Luther Says: An Anthology* (St Louis: Concordia, 1959), 560.
16. Thomas Hughes, *Tom Brown's Schooldays*, quoted in F. W. Boreham, *In Pastures Green: A Ramble through the Twenty-third Psalm* (London: Epworth, 1954), 46, 48.

different way, but it is all part of the same work, to the glory of God. So 'be steadfast, immovable, always abounding in the work of the Lord, knowing that in the Lord your labor is not in vain' (1 Cor. 15:58).

5

ALL IN GOOD TIME

He has made everything beautiful in its time. Also, he has put eternity into man's heart, yet so that he cannot find out what God has done from the beginning to the end.

Ecclesiastes 3:11

After everything else he has said about the vanity of our existence, we probably expect the Solomon of Ecclesiastes to say something discouraging about time too. He might say that the time is short, for example, and thus we never have enough time to do all the things we want to do. Or he might talk about the tyranny of time—the way it controls our lives down to the last millisecond. Plautus wrote about this. Bemoaning the stress caused by the latest timekeeping device of his era, the Roman playwright said: 'The gods confound the man … who has cut and hacked my days so wretchedly into small pieces. Confound him who in this place set up a sundial.'[1]

1. Plautus, quoted by A. Cornelius Gellius in his *Attic Nights (Noctes Atticae)*, Book 3, section 3.

What else might the Preacher who wrote Ecclesiastes say about time? He might say that time is fleeting, and that we are running out of time. Or he might say that once time is gone it can never be recovered, like the American educator Horace Mann, who once wrote the following want ad: 'Lost, yesterday, somewhere between Sunrise and Sunset, two golden hours, each set with sixty diamond minutes. No reward is offered, for they are gone forever.'[2] Or perhaps the mysteries of time would give Qoheleth the same anxious thoughts of insignificance that they gave the French philosopher Pascal:

> When I consider the short duration of my life, swallowed up in the eternity that lies before and after it, when I consider the little space I fill and I see, engulfed in the infinite immensity of spaces of which I am ignorant, and which know me not, I rest frightened, and astonished, for there is no reason why I should be here rather than there. Who put me here? Why now rather than then?[3]

A Time for This, A Time for That

These are all things that the Preacher might have said, but decided not to. Instead he celebrated the orderliness of God by writing the world's most famous poem on the subject of time. Long before the 1960s, when the Byrds sang their hit single 'Turn, Turn, Turn', Qoheleth's lyrics had struck a responsive chord in the human heart:

---

2. Horace Mann, quoted in Elizabeth M. Knowles, ed. *The Oxford Dictionary of Quotations*, 5th edition (Oxford: Oxford University Press, 1999), 493.

3. Pascal, *Pensées*, 78.

> For everything there is a season, and a time for every
> matter under heaven:
> a time to be born, and a time to die;
> a time to plant, and a time to pluck up what is planted;
> a time to kill, and a time to heal;
> a time to break down, and a time to build up;
> a time to weep, and a time to laugh;
> a time to mourn, and a time to dance;
> a time to cast away stones, and a time to gather stones
> together;
> a time to embrace, and a time to refrain from embracing;
> a time to seek, and a time to lose;
> a time to keep, and a time to cast away;
> a time to tear, and a time to sew;
> a time to keep silence, and a time to speak;
> a time to love, and a time to hate;
> a time for war, and a time for peace. (Eccles. 3:1-8)

Although everyone recognizes the beauty of these lines, some scholars believe that the poem's perspective is pessimistic. The Preacher is trapped in the tyranny of time and fatalistic about his time-bound existence. Thus, one commentary gives the following heading to Ecclesiastes 3: 'Hopelessness of Struggle against an Arbitrary God.'[4] On this reading, the God of Ecclesiastes is like the deity that the English poet and novelist Thomas Hardy wrote about—'the dreaming, dark, dumb Thing that turns the handle of this idle Show.'[5]

Remember, though, that chapter 2 ended with a declaration of the enjoyment we find wherever God is present and we

---

4. Frederick Carl Eiselen, ed., *Abingdon Bible Commentary* (New York: Doubleday, 1979).

5. Thomas Hardy, *The Dynasts* (1904, 1906, 1908).

receive life's blessings as a gift from Him. Notice as well the strong affirmation in verse 11: 'He has made everything *beautiful* in its time.' Far from becoming a fatalist, the Preacher has come to praise God's sovereignty over time and eternity as a thing of beauty.

Father Time

Notice that the Preacher locates all the times of life 'under heaven', which is more positive than his usual phrase, 'under the sun'. Everything in this time-bound universe is under the authority of God in heaven. The sovereign God rules over time and over what happens in time: 'For *everything* there is a season, and a time for *every* matter under heaven' (Eccles. 3:1, emphasis added). Nothing happens outside the will of God.

Qoheleth's poem emphasizes the scope of God's sovereignty with pairs of related opposites. Each pair forms a *merism*—a figure of speech in which two polarities make up a whole. Taken together, birth and death comprise the whole of human existence; weeping and laughing cover the full range of human emotion, and so on.

There is also something comprehensive about the entire list. There are fourteen pairs in all, which is twice the biblical number (seven) of perfection and completion. Furthermore, the pairs themselves take in the whole sweep of human experience, from birth to death, from war to peace, and everything in between.

God rules all our moments and all our days, and there is a definite orderliness to what He does. His sovereignty has a chronology. In the divine economy 'there is a season for everything'—a suitable occasion or appropriate opportunity for everything that happens. There is a time to matriculate, and a time to graduate; a time to take a job, and a time to retire; a time to stay, and a time to go home. Such a perspective is far from fatalistic. The Preacher is *not* saying that there is nothing we can do about what happens. His point rather is that there is a 'fittingness' to what happens. God does everything at just the right time.

People usually think of the actions in Ecclesiastes 3 as things that people do, which of course they are. We could demonstrate this from the life of King Solomon, who built great buildings, planted magnificent gardens and gathered many proverbs. But the activities listed in this poem are also things that *God* does. They are divine actions before they become human activities.

Consider birth and death—two appointments that every person must keep. Both the cradle and the grave follow God's timetable. A person's 'days are determined', Job said to his Creator, 'and the number of his months is with you' (Job 14:5). The Lord of life has sovereign power over death. The initiation, duration and termination of our earthly existence are all under His divine authority.

Some people would prefer a one-dimensional deity. They like to think of God as giving life, but not appointing the time of death. They would rather see God as planting and building than uprooting and tearing down. But God is not either/or. He is both/and, depending on what time it is.

Ecclesiastes 3 gives us the complete picture: to know God and to understand our place in His world we need to accept that both halves of each pair tell us the truth about His character. God makes 'time for every matter under heaven' because at the right time everything in this poem is fully in keeping with who He is: birth and death, mourning and laughter, love and hate, exclusion and embrace, war and peace.

Perfect Timing

The place where we see God's timeliness most clearly is in the person and work of Jesus Christ. In teaching us about the character of almighty God, this lyric also points us toward the Son who shares all divine perfections.

Jesus Christ is the Lord of time. As the Creator God He ordered the rhythms of creation. Now, by His resurrection from the dead, He rules the universe with sovereign authority over time and eternity. To borrow some evocative phrases from a classic hymn, He is 'the Lord of years' and 'the Potentate of time'.[6]

As we witness the life of Jesus in the Gospels we see a Savior who always knew what time it was. There was a time for Him to be born—just the right time, in fact. The Bible says that 'when the fullness of time had come, God sent forth his Son, born of woman' (Gal. 4:4). At just the right time—when the Gentiles were tired of serving the old pagan gods, when the Jews were weary of trying and failing to keep God's law, when the Greeks had given the world a common language, when the Romans had established (relatively) safe and easy travel across the Mediterranean—Jesus came with a message of salvation for the whole world.

There was also a day appointed for Jesus to die. He died on that particular day—not a day before, or a day after. For years people had plotted against Him, trying to put Him to death as soon as they could, yet 'his hour had not yet come' (John 7:30). When the hour did come, Jesus was crucified at Calvary, where He suffered for the vanity of all our sin. The Scripture says, 'at the right time Christ died for the ungodly' (Rom. 5:6). He rose again at the right time too: on the third day, as the Scriptures had promised (Hosea 6:2; cf. Luke 24:45-46; 1 Cor. 15:4). From His birth to His death and then on to His resurrection, Jesus did everything timely in His saving work. He was never late and never early, but always right on time.

---

6. Matthew Bridges, 'Crown Him with Many Crowns' (1852).

This is not surprising because, throughout His earthly ministry, Jesus always knew the right time for everything. He began His public ministry with the announcement that 'the time is fulfilled' (Mark 1:15). Then He proceeded to do everything at precisely the right moment. Jesus knew when it was time to plant and when it was time to uproot. When he said, 'I am the vine; you are the branches' (John 15:5), He was taking His disciples and replanting the ancient vineyard of the people of God. As Lord of the harvest He also said, 'Every plant that my heavenly Father has not planted will be rooted up' (Matt. 15:13). Jesus demonstrated this divine power when He cursed a fruitless fig tree: by the following morning, it had withered all the way down to its very roots (Mark 11:12-14, 20-21).

Jesus knew when it was time to heal. As He performed the miracles of the kingdom He made the lame to walk, the deaf to hear and the blind to see. Jesus knew when it was time to break down—think of the way He drove the moneychangers out of the temple, for example (Luke 19:45)—and also when it was time to build up, like the time He built His church on the rock of Peter's confession of the Christ (Matt. 16:15-18; cf. 7:24).

Jesus knew the right time for every emotion. There were times to mourn. The 'man of sorrows' (Isa. 53:3) grieved at the tomb of Lazarus (John 11:35, 38) and shed the Good Shepherd's tears for the lost sheep of Jerusalem (Luke 19:41-44; cf. Matt. 9:36). But there were also times for Him to dance with laughter. So, He rejoiced in the Holy Spirit when His disciples came back from their first mission trip and told Him how they had done the work of His joyful kingdom (Luke 10:21).

In personal relationships Jesus knew when it was time to seek for lost sheep and when it was time to lose the goats that refused to hear His voice. He embraced tax collectors, prostitutes and other poor sinners who knew how much they needed a Savior. But Jesus refrained from embracing the scribes, the Pharisees and other proud people who insisted that they were righteous enough for God.

Jesus knew when it was time to speak and when it was time to keep silent. He did a lot of talking—telling stories, explaining the law, preaching the gospel. But when it came time for the trial of His life, He did not speak in His own defense (Matt. 27:14) but suffered in silent innocence. Then it was time for Him to maintain silence, in fulfillment of the ancient prophecies: 'like a sheep he was led to the slaughter and like a lamb before its shearer is silent, so he opens not his mouth' (Acts 8:32; cf. Isa. 53:7; 1 Pet. 2:21-23).

To the day He died, Jesus knew the right time for everything. From beginning to end God's sovereignty over time and eternity is perfectly and gloriously displayed in the life and work of Jesus Christ.

Our Times, God's Hands

Jesus still knows what time it is. Do you believe this? He knows the time to love, showing mercy to needy sinners who ask Him to be their Savior. He knows the time to hate, standing against evil and injustice. He knows the time for war, as His church does battle against Satan and the enemies of God. Soon it will be time for peace, when He will 'make wars cease to the end of the earth' (Ps. 46:9), when He will set creation free from its bondage to the futility of our sin (Rom. 8:20-21) and we will never suffer again from the vanity of life under the sun.

In the meantime, Jesus calls us to make the best use of every moment. His lordship over time is not just for the big events of world history but also for our own everyday experiences. One of the best ways to avoid life's vanity is by knowing what to do with our time. The way we spend our time is the way we spend our lives. If we follow Jesus Christ then we need to know what time it is, not measuring time merely in terms of hours and days but viewing it as an opportunity for the service of God. There are at least three practical ways to apply this poem to the Christian life.

First, *wait for God's time*. If it is true that our Savior has perfect timing, then we should trust Him to know the right time for everything. King David was able to 'bless the LORD at all times' (Ps. 34:1) because he knew that whatever time it was, God was still in control. Most of us would prefer to manage our own agenda, which makes us quick to criticize God's timing. Instead of insisting on keeping our own timetable, we ought to hurry up and wait for God, as David did when he said, 'I trust in you, O LORD… . My times are in your hand' (Ps. 31:14,15).

Are you willing to put *your* times into God's hand? Consider the testimony of the pro-life activist Charmaine Crouse Yoest, who told *TIME* magazine about driving away from a party in tears because she was so lonely, not realizing that in the providence of God one of the people she met that night would become her husband.[7] Rather than thinking that God's timing is off, we should trust Him to know what He is doing all along.

Writing sometime in the fourth century after Christ, Didymus the Blind used a vivid example to explain why we should believe that God is in control. Didymus compared us to passengers on a large sailing vessel who have never met the captain, yet still believe that he is steering the ship. He

7. Charmaine Crouse Yoest, 'TIME for Thanks' (November 25, 2013) http://time100.time.com/2013/11/25/time-for-thanks/slide/charmaine-yoest/.

wrote: 'God himself manages the cosmos and looks after it... . When you see a ship which is piloted and holds its course, you perceive the idea of a helmsman even if he is not visible... . Likewise the Creator is known by his works and the order of his providence.'[8]

Second, *live your whole life knowing that there is a time for you to die*. The Bible says, 'it is appointed for man to die once, and after that comes judgment' (Heb. 9:27). Will you be ready when the time comes? Many people aren't. When the Vicomte de Turenne was mortally wounded at the Battle of Salzbach in 1675 he wistfully said, 'I did not mean to be killed today.'[9] By contrast, one 65-year-old widow from Amsterdam was totally prepared. After the death of her husband in 2005 she carefully planned her own funeral, including her choice of music. One day the following year, when she went to pay her respects where her husband was buried, she lay down and died right next to the family grave. The woman's name was already inscribed on the headstone, and her will was found inside her handbag.[10]

It would be hard for anyone to be better prepared to die than the Dutch woman was, although in truth anyone who trusts in Christ is ready to die at any time, because heaven is God's promise to every believer. Are you ready for eternity? If not, there is no time to lose. When it comes to receiving the free gift of eternal life in Jesus Christ, there is no time

---

8. Didymus the Blind, 'Commentary on Ecclesiastes', 88.29, *Proverbs, Ecclesiastes, Song of Solomon*, ed. by J. Robert Wright, Ancient Christian Commentary on Scripture, OT9 (Downers Grove, IL: InterVarsity, 2005), 230.
9. Vicomte de Turenne, quoted in Harold G. Moore and Joseph L. Galloway, *We Were Soldiers Once ... and Young* (New York: HarperCollins, 1992), 321.
10. This story was reported by Reuters on November 1, 2006.

like the present: 'Behold, now is the favorable time; behold, now is the day of salvation' (2 Cor. 6:2).

Redeeming the Time

Finally, *make good use of whatever time you have*. To use a memorable phrase from the apostle Paul, we should always be 'redeeming the time' (Eph. 5:16). As far as the Preacher was concerned, the best way to use time redemptively is to get busy in God-honoring ways. So, after reciting his poem he went on to say, 'there is nothing better for them than to be joyful and to do good as long as they live; also that everyone should eat and drink and take pleasure in all his toil—this is God's gift to man' (Eccles. 3:12-13).

It is not easy for us to use our time wisely. In this time-bound universe, where we are caught between time and eternity, the moments of our days are our most precious commodity. Time is the priceless currency that God has given for doing the work of His kingdom—what Stephen Olford has called 'a fragment of eternity given by God to man as a solemn stewardship.'[11] Time also happens to be one of the most difficult things for us to manage. We all have the same amount of time on a daily basis; the question is how we will spend it ... or whether we will waste it.

The best way to use our time is for the glory of God and the kingdom of Jesus Christ. This always requires deep spiritual wisdom. Even though we 'cannot find out what God has done from the beginning to the end' (Eccles. 3:11), we still have decisions to make every day. Later Qoheleth will say that 'the wise heart' is one that knows 'the proper time' (Eccles. 8:5). There are times in life to start something. But

11. Stephen F. Olford, *A Time for Truth: A Study of Ecclesiastes 3:1-8* (Chattanooga, TN: AMG, 1999), 9.

there are also times when something is supposed to come to an end—a project, a relationship, a ministry. Knowing the difference takes wisdom, because these are some of the hardest decisions in life.

If we want to have the heart of Jesus we need to know when it is time to 'weep with those who weep' or else 'rejoice with those who rejoice' (Rom. 12:15; cf. John 16:20). We need wisdom for the timing of our relationships, knowing when it is time to embrace someone and when it is time to exclude them from our plans and our priorities. There are times when it is important to speak up, saying a word in season (see Prov. 15:23; 25:11) or giving a reason for the hope that is in us (1 Pet. 3:15). But there are also times to shut up—times when silence is golden and it is better to hold our tongues (see Ps. 141:3; Prov. 27:14; James 1:26).

Redeeming the time requires wisdom in the use of our possessions. There are times to gather and times to scatter. There are times to keep something that we may need later, but also times to cast it away for someone else to use.

Who is sufficient for these things? If there is 'a time for every matter under heaven' (Eccles. 3:1), then redeeming the time will require wise decision-making. We must learn to ask God what time it is. Lord, is this a time to break down or build up? Is this something You want me to love or to hate? Am I speaking because I want to say something, or because I really have something to say? Ask God for help, and He will give you the wisdom to know what time it is (see James 1:5).

One day soon, Jesus will come again—'a second time' (Heb. 9:28), the Bible says. Indeed, Jesus will come at just the right time, at the precise hour His Father has appointed (Matt. 24:36). When that day comes time will be no more, and our deep longing for eternity will be satisfied. We will be with God forever. In the meantime, we are wise to pray the way that Moses prayed: 'teach us to number our days that we may get a heart of wisdom' (Ps. 90:12).

6

DEATH AND INJUSTICE

All go to one place. All are from the dust, and to dust all return.... Again I saw all the oppressions that are done under the sun. And behold, the tears of the oppressed, and they had no one to comfort them!

ECCLESIASTES 3:20, 4:1

Few contemporary writers are more highly regarded than Julian Barnes, the English essayist and novelist who wrote *Flaubert's Parrot*, *The Sense of an Ending* and other prize-winning books. In 2013 Barnes published *Levels of Life*, a poignant memoir that the author wrote after the death of his beloved wife. This followed an earlier memoir, in which he admitted that he was afraid to die. This confession was something of an embarrassment because, as an agnostic, Barnes honestly did not think that death was anything to be scared of. If there is no good reason to believe in God, he reasoned, and also no such thing as life after death, then there is (to use the title of his memoir) *Nothing to be Frightened Of.*

Yet, in the memoir Barnes frankly admitted that he *was* afraid to die—desperately afraid. *The New York Times*

Book Review correctly diagnosed the author's condition as *thanatophobia*, or the fear of death. Barnes admitted that he thinks about death every day and that sometimes in the night he is 'roared awake' and 'pitched from sleep into darkness, panic and a vicious awareness that this is a rented world.' Awake and utterly alone, he finds himself beating his pillow with a fist and wailing 'Oh no Oh No OH NO.'

Julian's dreams are even darker. Sometimes he is buried alive. Other times he is 'chased, surrounded, outnumbered'. He finds himself 'held hostage, wrongly condemned to the firing squad, informed that there is even less time' than he thought. 'The usual stuff,' he calls it.[1] And perhaps this *is* the usual stuff, because death is the sum of all our fears: of being alone, abandoned or condemned.

Man's Inhumanity to Man

When you wake up in the middle of the night, what are *you* afraid of?

Ecclesiastes faces up to all our fears by asking the hardest questions that anyone can ask about the meaning of the universe, the existence of God and the life to come. So far the Solomon of Ecclesiastes has tested the limits of human knowledge, attempted to do his moral duty, indulged in many pleasures and immersed himself in his work—trying anything and everything he can to make sense of his world.

At the end of chapter 3 the author deals with the difficult question of death. He had been thinking about all the injustice in the world and about his longing for God to make things right at the Final Judgment. But thinking about that

1. *Nothing to be Frightened Of* was published by Knopf in 2008. The quotations here come from Garrison Keillor, 'Dying of the Light', *The New York Times Book Review* (October 5, 2008), 1, 10.

great and terrible day naturally caused him to wonder what will happen when we die.

Try to follow Qoheleth's reasoning, beginning in 3:16: 'I saw under the sun that in the place of justice, even there was wickedness, and in the place of righteousness, even there was wickedness.' As we have seen before, the phrase 'under the sun' may be taken to describe 'the futility and meaninglessness of life lived only for self and the moment, without gratitude to or regard for God and his ways.'[2] What we see 'under the sun' in this instance is rampant injustice—what the Scottish poet Robert Burns famously called 'man's inhumanity to man'.[3]

Here Qoheleth sounds like one of the biblical prophets, crying for justice. This is one of the deepest longings of the human heart—an end to all the unfairness. The particular problem in this case is that even 'the place of justice' is unjust. The very place where people most need to receive justice turns out to be a locus of unfairness. Innocent people are convicted for crimes they never committed. They were in the wrong place at the wrong time, or maybe the wrong color on the wrong side of town. People lie, cheat and steal; sometimes they get away with murder. They have the money to hire better lawyers, or they hide behind the structure of some large institution to take advantage of people who are much less fortunate. It is all so unfair.

Even worse, there is nothing that can be done. The Preacher's frustration is that injustice goes unpunished. When the halls of justice become corridors of corruption, where can righteousness be found?

---

2. T. M. Moore, *Ecclesiastes: Ancient Wisdom When All Else Fails: A New Translation and Interpretive Paraphrase* (Downers Grove, IL: InterVarsity, 2001), 11.
3. Robert Burns, 'Man Was Made to Mourn: A Dirge' (1784).

The Preacher revisits this theme at the beginning of chapter 4, where he says: 'Again I saw all the oppressions that are done under the sun. And behold, the tears of the oppressed, and they had no one to comfort them! On the side of their oppressors there was power, and there was no one to comfort them' (Eccles. 4:1). By this reasoning, there are two kinds of people in the world: the oppressed and their oppressors. And, of course, the oppressors have all the advantages. The power is all on their side, leaving their victims with nothing but tears.

Understand that this is a conflict in which God takes sides. He is not for injustice, but stands against it with all His power. We see this again and again in the biblical prophets. Amos preached against people who 'oppress the poor' and 'crush the needy' (Amos 4:1). Ezekiel warned about the mistreatment of foreigners. Zechariah advocated for the protection of widows, orphans, travelers and the poor (Zech. 7:9-10).

In speaking on behalf of God in this, these Old Testament prophets address many sins that we see everywhere today as well: the poor getting poorer, immigrants struggling to find decent jobs, laws enforced unequally, school systems failing their children, husbands abusing their wives. Then there are the greater evils: genocide, terrorism, sex trafficking, street children. Oh, the injustice of it all!

When the Preacher saw what was happening he longed for someone to comfort the oppressed and dry their tears. In a culture of exploitation he wanted to console the victims of injustice. Twice he lamented that no one could offer any comfort.

We see the same holy response in the life of Jesus Christ. Jesus often reacted to oppression with lamentation, as we see in the tears He shed for the lost sheep of Israel

(Matt. 9:36). At the same time, Jesus treated their oppressors with indignation; think of the angry words He spoke to the moneychangers at the temple (e.g. Luke 19:45-46).

Caught somewhere between grief and anger, we feel the same frustration today. Consider the story of 'Lana', a 19-year-old Egyptian girl who was raised in a devout Muslim home. Lana had been taught to despise Christianity, but one day a friend from school invited her to listen to a radio program that proclaimed the gospel. The more she listened the more Lana began to doubt that Jesus was merely a messenger, as she had always been told. Eventually reading the Bible brought her to a clear conviction that Jesus Christ truly is the living God.

Sadly, when Lana accepted Jesus as her Savior and Lord, she was attacked by her family. Her father beat her. Her mother would no longer allow her to sit with her family at meals. Eventually they declared that Lana was dead to them. But even after they threw her out of the house they continued to persecute her. Her own family had her kidnapped and beaten until finally she was left broken and unconscious.[4]

This is what we see under the sun: persecution we are powerless to prevent. So how should we respond? How does all this suffering fit in with our theology? If God is good, why do so many bad things happen?

A Time for Justice

The writer of Ecclesiastes had a good answer to the problem of injustice. He said in his heart: 'God will judge the righteous and the wicked, for there is a time for every matter and for every work' (Eccles. 3:17).

---

4. Lana's story is recounted in a 2008 issue of *The Voice of the Martyrs*, 4-5.

Here we see the Preacher applying one of his own sermons to his own heart. He takes a spiritual principle that he taught earlier and applies it to the issue of injustice. If there is a season for everything and 'a time for every matter under heaven' (Eccles. 3:1), then there must be a time for justice. Therefore, rather than simply getting angry and sad about all the oppression we see in the world, we can trust God to make things right in the end.

This does not mean that there is never a time for us to pursue justice. Depending on our place in society—our position of privilege, our place of influence, and our God-given authority—it is our duty to fight against oppression in the church and in the wider world.

Yet even our best efforts will not bring an end to all oppression. There will still be violence against women and children, structures of corruption in business, government, and even law enforcement. But in all the situations that we do not have the power, the authority or the wisdom to resolve, God will see to it that justice is done.

Our confidence does not lie in a justice system but in the Chief Justice Himself: Jesus Christ. God has promised a day when His Son will judge the righteous and the wicked (Acts 17:30-31). The appointed time for His divine retribution is the Day of Judgment, when the Son of God will render His final verdict on humanity. 'Shall not the Judge of all the earth do what is just?' (Gen. 18:25). Indeed, the wicked will be punished forever (Matt. 25:41-46) and the righteous will be comforted by the Spirit of God, who will wipe every tear from their eyes (Rev. 21:4). As Solomon will go on to say at the very end of his book: 'God will bring every deed into judgment, with every secret thing, whether good or evil' (Eccles. 12:14).

Jesus Christ will bring final justice. Therefore, we live in the sure hope and certain expectation of His great day. Whenever we see injustice—acts of oppression that we are powerless to prevent—we pray for justice and then leave matters in God's hands. This takes faith in God's promises and patience to wait for His timing. Sometimes the only thing we can do is cry out, 'O Sovereign Lord, holy and true, how long before you will judge?' (Rev. 6:10). Yet Jesus has promised that when we pray day and night, God 'will give justice ... speedily' (Luke 18:8). If it seems a long time coming, we should remember the words of the prophets, who said: 'If it seems slow, wait for it; it will surely come; it will not delay' (Hab. 2:3).

Dust to Dust

Even if we believe that justice is coming we may still wonder why it is delayed. To be sure, God will make everything right in the end, but why doesn't He judge people right away? Why does He wait until the Day of Judgment?

The Preacher had a reasonable answer to this question as well: 'I said in my heart with regard to the children of man that God is testing them that they may see that they themselves are but beasts' (Eccles. 3:18).

Our present existence is a proving ground. It is a test, not simply in the sense of something we pass or fail, but also in the sense of something that demonstrates our true character.[5] One of life's purposes is to examine and ultimately to reveal our true relationship to God. This test is not for God's benefit, as if there were anything about us that he doesn't know already, but for our benefit, so that we recognize our mortality. Will we learn to see ourselves for who we really are? This is the searching question that waiting for justice poses for every one of us.

Ecclesiastes helps to clarify our identity by telling us that we are animals. This is not a comment on our biology, but

5. See Kidner, *Message of Ecclesiastes*, 42.

on our destiny. Here is how the Preacher explains it: 'For what happens to the children of man and what happens to the beasts is the same; as one dies, so dies the other. They all have the same breath, and man has no advantage over the beasts, for all is vanity. All go to one place. All are from the dust, and to dust all return' (Eccles. 3:19-20).

This is one of the Bible's strongest statements of the inevitability of death, which is the greatest of all equalizers. Animals are living creatures. Like us, they have been given life and breath by their Creator. But this life will not last forever. The day will come when each of us will breathe our last. With our parting breath each of us will go to the same place, returning to dust. By using this language the Preacher is reminding us of God's curse against Adam's sin: dust we are, and to the dust we shall return (Gen. 3:19). 'Ashes, ashes, we all fall down.' In this dog-eat-dog world, we are no better than animals.

Qoheleth will return to this theme again in chapter 6, when he compares our destiny unfavorably with the fate of a stillborn baby!

> If a man fathers a hundred children and lives many years, so that the days of his years are many, but his soul is not satisfied with life's good things, and he also has no burial, I say that a stillborn child is better off than he. For it comes in vanity and goes in darkness, and in darkness its name is covered. Moreover, it has not seen the sun or known anything, yet it finds rest rather than he. Even though he should live a thousand years twice over, yet enjoy no good—do not all go to the one place? (Eccles. 6:3-6).

How shall we respond to the dreadful certainty of our mortality? Are we better off dead? One order of Trappist monks digs a grave together. Every day they go to the gravesite, peer over the edge, and ponder their mortality. When one of them dies, they lower his body into the grave and cover him with dirt. Then they dig a new grave and start the ritual all over again, never knowing who will be the next to die.[6]

Not everyone responds to death in such a practical way. Some people try to laugh it off, like Woody Allen, who famously said, 'I am not afraid of death; I just don't want to be there when it happens!' But many people *are* afraid, like Julian Barnes. They have terrors in the night and despair of ever finding any lasting hope or authentic meaning in life. The Preacher is at that desperate point here; 'all is vanity', he says (Eccles. 3:19). If everyone dies, then life has no meaning. Just ask Livia Soprano, the television character who callously told her grandson, 'In the end, you die in your own arms. … It's all a big nothing'.[7]

Is there Life after Death?

For a moment it seemed as if the Final Judgment would solve the problem of injustice. But as it turns out, the solution was only temporary at best. As the Preacher reflected further on the delay of divine justice and started thinking about the implications of his mortality, he ended up right back where he started. Here we go again: vanity of vanities! Meaningless, meaningless; it's all meaningless.

Still, the Preacher knew of one thing that could make a difference in the face of death. Even if our bodies return to the dust, maybe our souls will live forever. This would give us some reassurance that oppressors will come to justice.

---

6. The practice of these monks is described by Haddon Robinson in 'The Grim Shepherd', *Christianity Today* (October 23, 2000), 115.

7. *The Sopranos,* Season 2, Episode 7 (2000).

The trouble was that he wasn't quite sure whether he believed in life after death: 'Who knows whether the spirit of man goes upward and the spirit of the beast goes down into the earth?' (Eccles. 3:21). Obviously, the Preacher had heard the conventional wisdom that when animals die they just die, but when people die their spirits rise to heaven. Yet he was starting to have his doubts. So, he asked the agnostic question: Who knows? Can we really be sure that after we die we will go to heaven and live with God?

This is the most basic question that we can ask about our destiny. We know that one day the time will come for us to die. The question is: Will we live again? Qoheleth was struggling to find certainty. 'Who knows?' he said.

As he wrestled with this doubt the Preacher's first impulse was to throw himself back into his work: 'So I saw that there is nothing better than that a man should rejoice in his work, for that is his lot. Who can bring him to see what will be after him?' (Eccles. 3:22). If we are facing an uncertain future, maybe the best thing we can do right now is to be productive.

But unless we have the assurance of eternal life, finding joy in our everyday work will never give us lasting satisfaction. We see this in the opening verses of chapter 4, where the Preacher spirals back down into despair. Witnessing ungodly oppression by evil men makes him envy the dead and the unborn: 'And I thought the dead who are already dead more fortunate than the living who are still alive. But better than both is he who has not yet been and has not seen the evil deeds that are done under the sun' (Eccles. 4:2-3; cf. 9:4-6).

Have you ever wished that you had never been born, or else wanted your life to end so that all your troubles would be over? These thoughts are tempting for everyone at one point or another. Given all of the depressing things that happen in this depraved world, maybe we would be better off dead.

From Dust to Glory

By this point it is clear that Ecclesiastes does not have all the answers. This frustrates scholars who see 'no progression of thought from one section to another' and who claim that Qoheleth 'offers no universal or satisfactory answer' to any of the problems he poses.[8] But at least this book asks the right questions! As well as anyone else in history, Qoheleth accurately identified the problems of human existence. If we continue to ask his questions and look for the answers that God has for us in the gospel, the Holy Spirit will lead us to the truth of everlasting life. One of the early church fathers rightly said that by 'instructing us through enigmas', Ecclesiastes 'guides us to the other life'.[9]

One way to find this life is by giving the full biblical answers to the questions that the Preacher raises in this passage—questions like, 'Who knows whether the spirit of man goes upward?' (Eccles. 3:21) and, 'Who can bring him to see what will be after him?' (Eccles. 3:22).

These are great questions. If we wanted to, we could answer some of them from Ecclesiastes. In the final chapter Qoheleth straightforwardly affirms that 'the dust returns to the earth as it was, and the spirit returns to God who gave it' (Eccles. 12:7). Clearly, he came to believe in life after death.

But the best answer of all is the one that God has given in Jesus Christ. Anyone who wants to know what will happen after death should ask Jesus, because He has been to the other side.

---

8. Whybray, *Ecclesiastes*, 17.

9. Olympiodorus, 'Commentary on Ecclesiastes', 3.21, in *Proverbs, Ecclesiastes, Song of Solomon*, ed. by J. Robert Wright, Ancient Christian Commentary on Scripture, OT 9 (Downers Grove, IL: InterVarsity, 2005), 233.

When Jesus was brought to the place of justice, there was no justice for Him at all.[10] There was no one to speak in His defense, no one to rescue Him from the deadly cross and no one to comfort Him when He was laid in the dust of death. But Jesus did not stay dead. On the third day, He rose again. His body and His spirit ascended to immortal glory. In the words of Dietrich Bonhoeffer, 'Christ lives. The trunk of the cross becomes the wood of life, and now in the midst of the world on the accursed ground itself, life is raised up anew. In the center of the world, from the wood of the cross, the fountain of life springs up.'[11]

The body and the spirit of the risen Christ have ascended to immortal glory. Now everyone who believes in Jesus will 'rise again to a better life' (Heb. 11:35). This is why we can be absolutely certain of eternal life. It is because Jesus brought eternal life out of the deadly grave. As the Scripture says, He 'abolished death and brought life and immortality to light through the gospel' (2 Tim. 1:10).

The Civil War correspondent Samuel Wilkerson claimed this great promise as he surveyed the carnage after the Battle of Gettysburg. In the providence of God the journalist discovered the body of his own son, who had fought for the Union and fallen in battle. In his overwhelming grief Wilkerson did not despair, but claimed the resurrection promise that those who die in Christ will rise again. Here is what he wrote for the *New York Times*, as he stood next to the body of his beloved son:

> Oh, you dead, who at Gettysburg have baptized with your blood the Second birth of Freedom in America, how you

10. This theme is developed nicely in Treier, *Proverbs & Ecclesiastes*, 159.
11. Dietrich Bonhoeffer, *Creation and Fall*, in *Dietrich Bonhoeffer, Works* (Minneapolis, MN: Augsburg Fortress, 2004), 3:146.

> are to be envied! I rise from a grave whose set clay I have passionately kissed, and I look up and see Christ spanning this battlefield with his feet and reaching fraternally and lovingly up to heaven. His right hand opens the gates of Paradise—with his left he beckons to those mutilated, bloody, swollen forms to ascend.[12]

Have you claimed this promise by the death and resurrection of Jesus Christ, that when you go down to the dust of death, you will rise again to glory? If so, then you have resurrection comfort in all your sorrows. You can rejoice in whatever good work God gives you to do as you wait for the Day of Judgment. You have faith and hope to persevere in the face of injustice and oppression.

Earlier in this chapter I told the story of 'Lana', a young Egyptian convert who was persecuted for her faith in Jesus Christ. When Lana was disowned by her family, what kept her from despair, very specifically, was her faith in life after death with Jesus. 'I'm in real danger,' she testified, 'but I trust God because He is alive. My comfort is that it is only a short time I'm spending here on earth, but there will be a long time that I'll spend with Him.... We know there will come a time when there will be no more sorrow or suffering. This is our hope in the Lord Jesus.'[13]

Yes, this is our hope in the Lord Jesus: after all our troubles and sorrows, He will raise us up to glory.

---

12. Samuel Wilkerson, quoted in Harry S. Stout, *Upon the Altar of the Nation: A Moral History of the Civil War* (New York: Viking-Penguin, 2006), 240-241.

13. *The Voice of the Martyrs*, 4-5.

7

SATISFACTION *NOT* GUARANTEED

He who loves money will not be satisfied with money, nor he who loves wealth with his income; this also is vanity.

Ecclesiastes 5:10

The Moneylender and His Wife—a famous painting by the Renaissance artist Quentin Massys—confronts us with the choice that everyone must make between God and money. The moneylender sits at home, with a measuring scale and a pile of money in front of him on the table, carefully assessing the value of a single coin.

Yet our eye is also drawn to the woman sitting next to him, the moneylender's wife. She is leafing through a Bible or a book of spiritual exercises, presumably bought by her wealthy husband. She is having her devotions, except that she seems to be distracted by the money. As she turns the page she looks up from the book, her gaze captivated by the coin in her husband's hand.

Massys painted this image to make a serious point. His adopted city of Antwerp had become a world center for business and trade. But Massys saw how easily money can pull our souls away from the worship of God.[1]

All of us feel this tension. We know that God demands our highest allegiance. We believe that nothing is more precious than the message of His gospel—the forgiveness of our sins and the free gift of eternal life through faith in Jesus Christ. Yet we are so easily distracted. Sometimes we find it more exciting to watch a movie or go online shopping than we do to listen to what God says in His Word.

Economic Injustice

The Solomon of Ecclesiastes wants to help us win our spiritual struggle with materialism by showing us the vanity of money. He starts with the economic injustice that people suffer from the sinful structures of society. In a moment he will make this personal, but he starts by talking about the whole political system: 'If you see in a province the oppression of the poor and the violation of justice and righteousness, do not be amazed at the matter, for the high official is watched by a higher, and there are yet higher ones over them' (Eccles. 5:8).

Here the Preacher sees something that we all see: oppression and injustice. We see it in communism, where the state seizes control of the means of production. But we also see it in capitalism whenever profit is pursued without regard for the well-being of other persons. Somehow poor people always seem to get the worst end of the bargain, and when this happens, Ecclesiastes tells us not to be surprised.

---

1. James Snyder, Larry Silver and Henry Luttikhuizen, *Northern Renaissance Art*, 2nd ed. (Upper Saddle River, NJ: Prentice Hall, 2005), 442. Wheaton College art historian Matt Milliner says that this point is made even more obviously in Marinus van Reymerswaele's 1539 version of Massys's image.

This is not to excuse unrighteousness; it is simply being realistic about life in a fallen world.

To make his point, Qoheleth refers to a hierarchy in which one person oversees another. Maybe the issue he has with hierarchy is the way it tends to become a tedious bureaucracy: call this the 'red tape' interpretation.[2] On this view, the verse is about 'the frustrations of oppressive bureaucracy with its endless delays and excuses, while the poor cannot afford to wait, and justice is lost between the tiers of the hierarchy.'[3]

Or perhaps the point is that each level of government takes something from the level below. Do not be surprised when people in authority abuse their power. Eventually injustice reaches all the way down to the poor, who probably would oppress someone if they could but can't because they're at the bottom. On this interpretation, the problem is not bureaucracy but tyranny.

Whichever interpretation we prefer, there are so many forms of injustice that we should never be surprised by sin. Our experience in this fallen world leads us to expect corruption at every level of government, right up to the very top. Although some leaders are motivated by a pure desire to serve society, many others are like the infamous Philadelphia politician who used public funds to sustain a lavish lifestyle and then boasted to his friends that he was spending 'Other People's Money'.

The best governments assume from the outset that people are sinners and that therefore need checks and balances to restrain unrighteousness. But even the best governments are far from perfect. As long as we live on God's green earth we will see people buying their way to power, using public

2. Longman III, *Book of Ecclesiastes*, 157.

3. Eaton, *Ecclesiastes*, 101.

position for personal gain and manipulating the system for their own advantage.

The Vanity of Prosperity

Up to this point Qoheleth has been talking about wealth and poverty on the national scale but, beginning in verse 10, he brings things down to the personal level. Public officials are not the only people who want to get more money; this is a temptation for all of us. So, the Preacher warns us about the vanity of prosperity: 'He who loves money will not be satisfied with money, nor he who loves wealth with his income; this also is vanity' (Eccles. 5:10; cf. 6:7).

Here we have a well-known truth, stated as a proverb, to which the Preacher adds his usual editorial comment about vanity. No matter how much money they have, people who live for money are never satisfied. Typically, they can relate to the title that Rabbi Harold Kushner gave to his book on Ecclesiastes: *When All You've Ever Wanted Isn't Enough.*[4] John D. Rockefeller was the richest man in the world, but when someone asked him how much money was enough, he famously said, 'Just a little bit more.' To use a more recent example, the television character Homer Simpson once said to his boss, Mr Burns, 'You're the richest man I know.' To which the wealthy magnate replied, 'Yes, but I'd trade it all for more.'

The contemporary author Jessie O'Neill has diagnosed this spiritual problem correctly. She calls it 'affluenza', which is 'an unhealthy relationship with money' or the pursuit of wealth.[5] Most Americans have at least a mild case of this

4. Rabbi Harold Kushner, *When All You've Ever Wanted Isn't Enough* (New York, Simon and Schuster, 2002).

5. Jessie O'Neill explains the term in her book *The Golden Ghetto: The Psychology of Affluence* (Center City, MN: Hazelden, 1996).

deadly disease, and people who live in the United States for a little while are likely to catch it too. Even if we are thankful for what we have, we often think about the things that we do not have and about how to get them. This explains the sudden pang of discontent we feel when we realize that we cannot afford something we want to buy, or else the guilt we feel because we bought it anyway. Call it 'acquisition without satisfaction'.

The appetite for what money can buy is never satisfied, and thus the only way to curb this reckless desire is to be content with what God provides. Charles Bridges said that when our desires run ahead of our needs it is better for us 'to sit down content where we are, than where we hope to be in the delusion of our insatiable desire.'[6] It is not just the love of money that causes us to be dissatisfied, either. Academic success, athletic victory, musical accomplishment, sexual pleasure—many good things in life may tempt us to have what Qoheleth calls a 'wandering appetite' (Eccles. 6:9). But rather than always craving more, we should be happy with less because we are satisfied with Jesus.

For many people the quest for contentment is a lifelong struggle. The fact that we have resisted the temptation of money before does not make us immune from it today. One day we may say, 'I don't care too much for money.' But soon we are singing a different tune, as the Beatles did: 'Money don't get everything, it's true / What it don't get, I can't use. / Now give me money (that's what I want).'[7]

---

6. Charles Bridges, *A Commentary on Ecclesiastes* (1860; repr. Edinburgh: Banner of Truth, 1961), 115.

7. From the songs 'Can't Buy Me Love' and 'Money' (That's What I Want) on the *Hard Day's Night* (1964) and *With the Beatles* (1963) albums, respectively.

Ecclesiastes warns us that living for things that only money can buy is vanity. To help us avoid coming down with a bad case of 'affluenza', the book gives us a long list of reasons why the pursuit of money will always leave us spiritually bankrupt.

One problem with money is that *other people will try to take it from us*. 'When goods increase,' the Preacher says, 'they increase who eat them, and what advantage has their owner but to see them with his eyes?' (Eccles. 5:11). This verse refers in some way to people who consume our wealth. It might be the oppressive government described in verses 8 and 9, which takes away our money through higher taxes. It might be our children—the hungry mouths around our dinner table. Or it might be the freeloaders who come begging for us to give them something for nothing. But no matter who these people are, the more we have, the more they try to get it.

No one knew this better than King Solomon. He was the richest man in the world, but with thousands of people to feed (see 1 Kings 4:22-28), he almost needed to be! Here he warns us that the more we have, the more people will want it. And if they get it from us, we will never be able to enjoy it for ourselves. This is vanity, as Solomon later reiterates: 'There is an evil that I have seen under the sun, and it lies heavy on mankind: a man to whom God gives wealth, possessions and honor, so that he lacks nothing of all that he desires, yet God does not give him power to enjoy them, but a stranger enjoys them. This is vanity; it is a grievous evil' (Eccles. 6:1-2).

Another problem with having more money is that *it will keep us awake at night*. The Preacher-King makes this point by drawing a contrast: 'Sweet is the sleep of a laborer, whether he eats little or much, but the full stomach of the rich will not let him sleep' (Eccles. 5:12).

As a general rule, people who work hard all day—especially if they work with their hands—are ready for a good night's sleep. The idle rich do not enjoy this luxury, but are up all night. In this case, their insomnia is caused by indigestion. Their gluttonous diet of fatty foods gives them a tummy-ache.

Having a lot of money can be very unhealthy—not just spiritually, but also physically. People who work hard should count their blessings, even if they cannot always count on getting a fat paycheck. Refreshing sleep is the blessing of manual labor. But the lifestyle of the rich and lazy tends not to be very restful. Derek Kidner looks at all our 'modern exercise-machines and health clubs' and concludes that it is 'one of our human absurdities to pour out money and effort just to undo the damage of money and ease.'[8]

Temporary Prosperity

So far, Qoheleth has been talking about the vanity of *having* a lot of money. In verses 13-14, he talks about the vanity of *losing* it: 'There is a grievous evil that I have seen under the sun: riches were kept by their owner to his hurt, and those riches were lost in a bad venture. And he is father of a son, but he has nothing in his hand.'

This is a third reason why living for money is meaningless: *it is here today, but it may be gone tomorrow.* To make this point, Qoheleth provides a case study, possibly based on personal acquaintance. A certain man tried to hoard his wealth, but lost it all in some risky investment. Today people lose their money in places like the stock market. In those days, their ships foundered at sea, or their camel trains were attacked in the wilderness. Whatever the reason, this man

---

8. Kidner, *Message of Ecclesiastes*, 56.

took a gamble, suffered a reversal of fortune, and ended up destitute.

Even worse, the man was a father, and now he had nothing to leave his son. The story assumes what the Bible teaches in other places (e.g. Prov. 13:22): fathers and mothers have a duty to save and sacrifice so that they are able to leave a legacy for their sons and daughters.

Not only did the man in the story fail to fulfill his fatherly duty, but in the end he lost all his money: 'As he came from his mother's womb he shall go again, naked as he came, and shall take nothing for his toil that he may carry away in his hand. This also is a grievous evil: just as he came, so shall he go, and what gain is there to him who toils for the wind?' (Eccles. 5:15-16).

The language of these verses is familiar to anyone who knows the story of Job. When that poor man lost everything, he said, 'Naked I came from my mother's womb, and naked shall I return. The LORD gave, and the LORD has taken away; blessed be the name of the LORD' (Job 1:21). The apostle Paul took the same truth and applied it to all of us: 'We brought nothing into the world, and we cannot take anything out of the world' (1 Tim. 6:7).

One day, all our labors will be lost. This is the tragic reality that every one of us must face. At the end of one of his most profitable years on the European Tour, someone asked the English golfer Simon Dyson if there was anything he was afraid of. 'Death,' Dyson replied. 'I'm in a position now where I can pretty much do as I want.... Dying wouldn't be good right now.'[9]

Whether or not we make as much money as a professional golfer, the day will come when we have to leave it all behind.

---

9. Simon Dyson, quoted in John Blanchard, *Where Do We Go from Here?* (Darlington, UK: Evangelical Press, 2008), 6.

We are here today, but we will be gone tomorrow. So, what gain is there in living for money? Some people wait until their deathbed to raise that question—if then!—but if we are wise like Solomon we will try to figure out the answer now. When Martin Luther considered the long-term value of his financial position, he proclaimed, 'As I shall forsake my riches when I die, so I forsake them while I am living.'[10] Luther didn't want to wait until he died; he wanted to get ready for that momentous day by letting go of his possessions while he was still alive.

What should we say about the things that we own? If we are wise, we will say to ourselves, 'Now here is something that God has given me to enjoy for the time being, or maybe to give away for the work of His kingdom, but I need to remember that I will never be able to take it with me when I die.' Since we are headed for eternity, we should travel light!

Many of Qoheleth's reasons to resist living for money are summarized in the comment that he makes about the wealthy person in verse 17: 'Moreover, all his days he eats in darkness in much vexation and sickness and anger.' This is where greed will lead. The miser will end up alone in his misery, living in spiritual darkness and vexed with many anxieties. The ungodly pursuit of wealth will take a physical toll, leaving him in poor health. He will also be very angry—a bitter old man. After all, who ever heard of a happy miser?

This verse gives us a helpful question to ask about our own anger, some of which may well be caused by excessive love for the things of this world. When we get angry, what is the reason? Upon reflection, we will discover that our unsatisfied desire for worldly possessions is a prevalent and powerful producer of anger.

---

10. Martin Luther, 'Notes on Ecclesiastes', in *Luther's Works*, 15:91.

The Power to Enjoy

Happily, there is a better way to live. Ecclesiastes says it like this: 'Behold, what I have seen to be good and fitting is to eat and drink and find enjoyment in all the toil with which one toils under the sun the few days of his life that God has given him, for this is his lot. Everyone also to whom God has given wealth and possessions and power to enjoy them, and to accept his lot and rejoice in his toil—this is the gift of God' (Eccles. 5:18-19).

Some scholars find these verses so completely contrary to what the Preacher has just said that they think he must be speaking sarcastically. Qoheleth does not *really* believe that life is very enjoyable, but he is trying to help us enjoy it while we can. So he tells us to eat, drink and be industrious, for tomorrow we die.

That is not all the Preacher says, however. He gives us a balanced, God-centered view. Just as he has been honest about the vanity of prosperity, he also wants to tell the truth about finding joy in the everyday things of life, such as working and feasting. This is a recurring theme in Ecclesiastes; we see it in the so-called 'enjoyment passages' that appear throughout the book (e.g. 2:24-26). Qoheleth knows that joy is real because he has experienced it for himself. Yes, our time on earth is short, but whatever time we have left is a sacred gift. When the Preacher calls our lives 'the gift of God', this is not sarcasm but godly gratitude.

The Preacher can say this because he believes in the God of joy. Earlier, when he was talking about the vanity of money, he hardly mentioned God at all. But in verses 18 to 20, he mentions Him repeatedly. Evidently, whatever enjoyment he finds is God-centered. Without God, life is meaningless and miserable, especially if we live for money. But when we know the God of joy, even money can be a blessing.

Notice the phrasing of verse 19. Earlier, the Preacher listed some of the many reasons why money is vanity. Yet here he tells us explicitly that if we are wealthy, we should enjoy it. This almost sounds like a contradiction, but notice where the power of enjoyment originates: it comes from God. Both having things and enjoying things are gifts from God. When the God of joy is with us, even money can prove to be a blessing. On the other hand, if God is absent, then nothing can satisfy us, least of all money. As the poet Christian Wiman has observed, 'if God has no relationship to your experience, if God is not *in* your experience, then experience is always an end in itself … a dead end.'[11]

This profound insight helps us take a balanced view of our earthly possessions. The world that God created is full of many rich gifts, but the power to enjoy them does not lie in the gifts themselves. This is why it is always useless to worship the gifts instead of the Giver. The ability to enjoy wealth, or food, or friendship, or work, or sex, or any other good gift comes only from God. Satisfaction, so to speak, is sold separately. Thus, the person who finds the greatest enjoyment in life is the one who has a close, personal relationship with the Giver. Charles Bridges spoke from a place of spiritual intimacy when he testified, 'I have found more in Christ than I ever expected to want.'[12]

The English poet George Herbert explored the power of enjoyment in his poem 'The Pulley'.[13] Herbert began by saying that when God first made man, He took his glass and poured out as much blessing as He could: riches, beauty,

---

11. Christian Wiman 'God's Truth Is Life' (from *My Bright Abyss*), *SEEN* (Christians in the Visual Arts), 13:2 (2013), 8.
12. Bridges, *Commentary on Ecclesiastes*, 66.
13. George Herbert, *George Herbert and the Seventeenth-Century Religious Poets*, ed. by Marion A.D. Cesare (New York: Norton, 1978), 57.

wisdom, honor and pleasure. But when the glass was almost empty, he decided to stop pouring. 'When almost all was out,' Herbert wrote, 'God made a stay, / Perceiving that alone of all his treasure / Rest in the bottom lay.' In other words, the one gift that God decided not to grant humanity was rest (or, we could say, satisfaction): 'For if I should (said he) / Bestow this jewel also on my creature, / He would adore my gifts instead of me.' In wisdom and love, God decreed that we should be 'rich and weary', so that tedium and fatigue would turn our hearts back to Him.

Have you turned away from the weariness of wealth and every other good thing to find your joy in God? Anyone who does not have joy in life must be looking in the wrong place. The way to find the joy is to pray, 'Lord, you know how empty I feel right now. Help me turn away from all the things I am using to fill the empty spaces in my life and fill me with your grace instead.'

The Preacher teaches us to depend on God for our joy, rather than depending on any one of God's many gifts. This is part of his answer to the problem of life's vanity. The person who learns this lesson well 'will not much remember the days of his life because God keeps him occupied with joy in his heart' (Eccles. 5:20). When we learn to enjoy God we experience so much joy that life's short vanity is all but forgotten.[14]

Quentin Massys appears to have learned this spiritual lesson. We see this in a detail from *The Moneylender and His Wife* that is as subtle as it is striking. Remember that in the masterpiece both husband and wife are tempted to turn away from God to focus on their money. On the table between them Massys cleverly painted a small round mirror, which reflects a little scene that takes place just outside the frame of

14. Eaton, *Ecclesiastes*, 104.

the painting. If we look at this small mirror image, we see the dark lines of a window-frame intersecting to make the form of a cross. We also see a small figure reaching out for the frame, as if to hold on to the cross. It might be Massys himself.

The artist—like the Preacher-King who wrote Ecclesiates—seems to be reminding us not to look for money to give us any satisfaction in life. Instead, we are invited to reach out for the cross where Jesus gave His life for all our greedy sins. If you hold on to the Savior, you will find full satisfaction in Him, guaranteed.

8

THE CROOK IN THE LOT

Consider the work of God: who can make straight what he has made crooked?

Ecclesiastes 7:13

Maybe your life is so carefree that you have been untouched by human suffering. Then again, maybe not. Maybe you have had to deal with a lot of brokenness: chronic illness, depression, anxiety, personal betrayal, broken relationships, false allegations, destructive sins, bereavement or sorrow.

Some of these are my struggles, and some are the struggles of people I love. I can relate to the young woman who was in a serious car accident and during her long recovery wrote about the days 'when you feel like a quivering, cowardly shell of yourself, when despair yawns as a terrible chasm, when fear paralyzes any chance for pleasure.'[1] The words 'Help me, Jesus!' come up frequently in my prayer life. So do prayers

1. Catherine Woodiwiss, quoted in David Brooks, 'The Art of Presence', *New York Times* (January 20, 2014).

from the Gospels such as 'Have mercy, Jesus, Son of David!' (Luke 18:38).

In times of trial I sometimes reflect on lessons I have learned from the Scottish theologian Thomas Boston, who pastored a little country church in the early 1700s. I studied Boston's writing for my doctoral work, so I feel like I know him well. In his *Memoirs* the man opens his heart to share his sufferings as well as the lessons he learned from them.

To put Boston's experiences into context, it is important to know that of the ten children who were born to Thomas and his wife Katherine, six died in their infancy. One loss was especially tragic. Boston had already lost a son named Ebenezer, which in the Bible means 'Hitherto hath the Lord helped us' (1 Sam. 7:12 KJV). When his wife was expecting another child, he considered naming the new child Ebenezer as well. Yet he hesitated. Naming the boy Ebenezer would be a testimony of hope in the faithfulness of God. But what if this child died, too, and the family had to bury another Ebenezer? This would be a loss too bitter to bear.

After wrestling with these thoughts in prayer, Boston decided by faith to name his son Ebenezer. Yet the child was born sickly, and despite the urgent prayers of his parents, he never recovered. As the grieving father wrote in his *Memoirs*, 'it pleased the Lord that he also was removed from me.'[2]

After suffering such a heavy loss many people would be tempted to accuse God of wrongdoing, abandon their faith, or at least drop out of ministry for a while. But that is not what Thomas Boston did. He believed in the goodness as well as the sovereignty of God. Rather than turning *away*

2. Thomas Boston, *The Complete Works of the Late Rev. Thomas Boston of Ettrick*, ed. by Samuel M'Millan, 12 vols. (London, 1853; repr. Wheaton, IL: Richard Owen Roberts, 1980), 12:205.

from the Lord in his time of trial, he turned *toward* the Lord for help and comfort.

Later, Boston preached a classic sermon on the sovereignty of God called *The Crook in the Lot.*[3] The sermon was based on the command that Qoheleth gives and the question he raises in Ecclesiastes 7:13: 'Consider the work of God: who can make straight what he has made crooked?'

Good Days, Bad Days

The command here is to 'consider'—to make a careful observation of the way God works. The Solomon who wrote Ecclesiastes noticed the world around him. He studied the seasons of life, learning when it was time for this and time for that. He watched the way people worked and played. He saw how they lived and died. Here in chapter 7 he invites us to join him by considering God's work in the world.

Then the Preacher asks a rhetorical question: Who can straighten out what God has made crooked? The answer, of course, is no one. Things are the way that God wants them to be; we do not have the ability to overrule the Almighty.

When the Preacher talks about something 'crooked' he is talking about some trouble we have in life we wish that we could change, but cannot. It happens to all of us. We struggle with physical limitations. We suffer the breakdown of personal or family relationships. We have something that we wish we did not have, or do not have something that we wish we did. Sooner or later, there is something in life that we wish to God had a different shape to it. What is the one thing in your life that you would change, if you had the power to change it?

According to Ecclesiastes, God has given each of us a different situation in life—our 'lot' in life (e.g. Eccles. 5:18,

3. Thomas Boston, *The Crook in the Lot*, in *Complete Works*, 3:495-590.

19). Thomas Boston used the same language when he wrote: 'There is a certain train or course of events, by the providence of God, falling to every one of us during our life in this world: and that is our lot, allotted to us by the sovereign God.'

Furthermore, we all have circumstances we wish that we could change. Boston continues:

> In that train or course of events, some fall out *cross* to us, and against the grain; and these make *the crook* in our lot. While we are here, there will be cross events, as well as agreeable ones, in our lot and condition. Sometimes things are softly and agreeably gliding on; but, by and by, there is some incident which alters that course … and pains us… . Everybody's lot in this world has some crook in it… . There is no perfection here.[4]

When some people hear Ecclesiastes speak along these lines they assume that Qoheleth is a fatalist. Some things are straight in life; other things are crooked. But whether they are crooked or straight there is absolutely nothing we can do about it. It all comes down to fate, or maybe predestination.

Qoheleth seems to take a similarly gloomy view in chapter 9, where he writes, 'Again I saw that under the sun the race is not to the swift, nor the battle to the strong, nor bread to the wise, nor riches to the intelligent, nor favor to those with knowledge, but time and chance happen to them all' (Eccles. 9:11). The English novelist and essayist George Orwell once offered a clever paraphrase of this verse: 'Objective considerations of contemporary phenomena compel the conclusion that success or failure in competitive activities exhibits no tendency to be commensurate with

4. Boston, *Crook in the Lot*, 3:499.

innate capacity, but that a considerable element of the unpredictable must invariably be taken into account.'[5] In other words, life is totally unpredictable. Whatever happens, happens.

There is another way to look at these verses, however. On an alternative reading, the Preacher is saying that whether things seem crooked or straight, we need to see our situation in terms of the sovereign goodness of God. If there is a crook in our lot, it is the work of God, which it would be vain for us to try and change.

One way to see the difference between despairing of our fate and hoping in God is to compare Ecclesiastes 7:13 to what the author said back in Ecclesiastes 1:15. The wording of the earlier verse is almost identical: 'What is crooked cannot be made straight.' Notice, however, that the first time the Preacher made this statement (or cited this proverb, perhaps), he left God out of the picture. He was giving us what C. S. Lewis accurately described as 'a clear, cold picture of man's life without God.'[6] But here in chapter 7 the Preacher brings God back into the picture. He looks at the world according to God, and puts both the straight things and the crooked things under His divine care.

It is still true that there is nothing we can do to straighten out what is crooked. We cannot change what God has done unless and until He wants to change it. We do not have the power to edit God's agenda. But far from driving us to despair, the sovereignty of God gives us hope through all the trials of life. We do suffer the frustration of life in a fallen

5. George Orwell, 'Politics and the English Language' (1946), quoted in Helen Sword, 'Inoculating Against Jargon', *The Chronicle Review* (June 8, 2012), B13.

6. C. S. Lewis, *Reflections on the Psalms* (New York: Harcourt, 1986), 115.

world. But the Bible promises us that God has a plan to set us free from all this futility, and that as He carries out this plan He is working all things together for our good (see Rom. 8:20, 28).

Trusting in the sovereign goodness of God helps us know how to respond to both the joys and the trials of life. Whether we are having a good day or a bad day, there is always some way for us to glorify God. So the Preacher says, 'In the day of prosperity be joyful, and in the day of adversity consider: God has made the one as well as the other' (Eccles. 7:14).

This perspective puts today and every day under the sovereignty of God. Some days are full of prosperity. The sun is shining, the birds are singing, and all is right with the world. Every good day, every tasty meal, every financial windfall, every meaningful conversation, every simple pleasure, every success in ministry—every blessing of any kind at all is a gift from God's grace that calls us to joy.

Not every day is like that, of course. Some days are full of adversity rather than prosperity. The sun is not shining, the birds are not singing, and nothing seems right with the world. It looks like our trials will never end, and we wonder if we have even one single friend in the world.

Yet this day too comes from the hand of God; it is under His sovereign care. The Preacher does not have the heart to tell us to be joyful on such a difficult day, but he does call us to consider the ways of God. When adversity comes, we should recognize that this too is a day that the Lord has made.

When we entrust every day of our lives to the loving care of a sovereign God, then we will be ready for anything and everything that life throws at us. In his comments on this verse Martin Luther advised: 'Enjoy the things that are present in such a way that you do not base your confidence on them, as though they were going to last forever. ... but reserve part of our heart for God, so that with it we can bear the day of adversity.'[7]

Whatever trials we have in life, it helps to go through them with Jesus at our side. If we are wise, we will offer whatever joys we experience back to God in thanksgiving. This is all part of what it means to *consider* the work of God. The Preacher is telling us to do something more than simply see what God has done. He is telling us to accept what God has done and surrender to His sovereign will, praising Him for all our prosperity and trusting Him through every adversity.

Two Dangers That Lead to Destruction

If the Preacher's perspective seems a little simplistic so far, a little too easy, then we can probably relate to what the Preacher says next. No sooner has he told us to consider the works of God than he struggles with God's sovereignty.

Remember, Qoheleth promised that he was totally committed to telling us the truth about life. What he tells us here is that sometimes life can be desperately unfair. 'In my vain life I have seen everything,' he says. 'There is a righteous man who perishes in his righteousness, and there is a wicked man who prolongs his life in his evildoing' (Eccles. 7:15).

This is exactly the opposite of what most people expect. The righteous people ought to rejoice in their prosperity, while the wicked suffer adversity until finally they admit that God is in control. All too often, what we see instead is what the Preacher saw: righteous people dying before their time while their enemies keep on living. Godly pastors are martyred for their faith while their persecutors live

7. Martin Luther, 'Notes on Ecclesiastes', in *Luther's Works*, 15:120.

to terrorize the church another day. Innocent victims get cut down in the prime of life, yet their attackers never get caught. It's just not fair!

These are some of the crooked things in life that we wish we could straighten out. But since we can't, the Preacher gives us some practical advice: 'Be not overly righteous, and do not make yourself too wise. Why should you destroy yourself? Be not overly wicked, neither be a fool. Why should you die before your time?' (Eccles. 7:16-17)

Some scholars believe that these verses are cynical, and maybe they are. Maybe the Preacher is saying: 'Look, if the righteous perish, while the wicked live to prosper, then don't try to be a goody two-shoes. If only the good die young, then there is nothing to be gained by trying to be good.'

This happens to be the way many people think today. They know better than to live a life of total wickedness, because deep down they believe that God will judge people for their sins. Yet, secretly, they suspect that trying to be holy will take the fun out of life, and they hope that they are good enough to get by on the Day of Judgment. As long as they are not too righteous, or too wicked, they are happy just the way they are.

If this is what the Preacher means then he must be looking at life under the sun again, leaving God out of the picture for the moment and thinking about good and evil the way that only an unbeliever can.

There is an alternative reading, however. When he tells us not to be 'overly righteous', he might be telling us not to be *self*-righteous. The form of the verb that the Preacher uses in verse 16 may refer to someone who is only pretending to be righteous.[8] After all, if God's standard is perfection—if

8. Whybray, *Ecclesiastes*, 120-21.

we are called to love Him with all our heart, soul, mind and strength—then how could anyone ever be 'overly righteous'? Our tendency is to think that we are more righteous than we really are, and this is a real problem.

To help us avoid thinking of ourselves too highly, the Preacher warns us not to be—so to speak—'too righteous'. We should never think that we are too good to suffer, or that it would be unfair for someone like us to have a crook in our lot. Yet it is often tempting to say, 'God, I don't deserve this. Don't you know who I am?' And it is only a short step from there to saying, 'Who does God think He is?'

This is not to say that we should be *un*righteous, of course. The Preacher warns against this mistake in verse 17, when he tells us not to be too wicked. His point here is *not* that it is okay for us to be a little bit wicked, as if there could ever be some tolerable level of iniquity. The Preacher's point rather is that there is great danger in giving ourselves over to evil. It is one thing to sin from time to time, as everyone does. The Preacher will say as much in verse 20: 'Surely there is not a righteous man on earth who does good and never sins.' But there is a world of difference between committing the occasional sin and making a deliberate decision to pursue a lifestyle of theft, deception, lust or greed. 'Don't be a fool,' the Preacher is saying. 'If you live in sin, you will perish.'

Thus, there are two dangers for us to avoid: *self*-righteousness and *un*righteousness. Both errors will lead to destruction; they may even lead to an untimely death. But there is a way to avoid both dangers, and that is to live every day in the fear of God: 'for the one who fears God shall come out from both of them' (Eccles. 7:18).

To fear God is to know that He is God and we are not. It is to hold Him in awe for His majestic beauty. It is to have respect for His mighty and awesome power. This helps us not to pretend to be something that we're not. It also keeps us from living a wicked life, because when we understand God's holiness the last thing we will want to do is fall under His righteous judgment.

Why God Allows Suffering

When we really do fear God, it will help us look beyond our present difficulties and see the work of God, accepting all the crooked things in our lives until He chooses to make them straight.

Earlier I mentioned Thomas Boston and his classic sermon on Ecclesiastes 7:13. Boston ended that sermon by listing some of the many reasons why God makes some things crooked.[9] These were biblical lessons that the man had confirmed through his own experience of grief and pain. Why does God leave some things crooked, even when we pray for Him to make them straight?

First, Boston said, the crooked things in life are a test *to help us determine whether we really are trusting in Christ for our salvation*. Think of Job, for example, who was afflicted with many painful trials in order to prove the genuineness of his faith. Our own sufferings may have the same purpose: by the grace of God, they confirm that we are holding on to Christ (or else help us see that we still need to trust Him for our salvation).

Second, God carefully designs whatever crooks we have in our earthly lot *to turn our hearts away from this vain world and teach us to look for happiness in the life to come*. Suffering is part of our preparation for eternity. Consider the Prodigal Son, who did not return to his father until he lost everything he had. His sufferings were part of a pilgrimage that led him back home,

---

9. Boston, *Crook in the Lot*, 3:511-16.

where he belonged. When something in life seems crooked, remember that a day is coming when God will make it straight.

Third, God uses the crooked things in life *to convict us of our sins*. The reason that anything is crooked at all is because there is sin in the world, including our own iniquity. The Holy Spirit often takes the crooks in our lot and uses them to touch our conscience, reminding us of some particular sin that we need to confess. It would be a mistake to think, every time we suffer, that this must be because of our sins. But it would also be a mistake to miss the opportunity that every trial brings to repent for any unconfessed sin.

Fourth, God may use the crooked things in life *to correct us for our sins*. There are times when suffering serves as an instrument of God's justice. So it was for David, after he had murdered Uriah: God justly decreed that the sword would never depart from his house (see 2 Sam. 12:10). When we suffer it may be because, as a consequence for our sin, we are under the judgment or the discipline of God.

These are not the only reasons why God makes some things crooked. Thomas Boston listed several others. Sometimes God allows us to suffer in order to keep us from committing a sin, or else to uncover a sinful attitude of the heart so deep that it could only be revealed by suffering a painful trial. Or maybe—and this is the happiest reason of all—God puts a crook into our lot in order to display His grace through our godliness under trial. We are prone to what Boston called 'fits of spiritual laziness'. But when we have a crook in our lot, it rouses us from our spiritual slumber and produces 'many acts of faith, hope, love, self-denial, and other graces.'[10]

---

10. Boston, *Crook in the Lot*, 3:515-16.

The Shepherd's Crook

The point of listing these possible reasons for our suffering is not to suggest that we can always figure out why God has put some particular crook in our lot. The point rather is that *God* knows why He has put it there. When something in life seems crooked, we are usually quick to tell God how He should straighten it out. Instead, we should let God straighten *us* out! In His sovereignty over our suffering, God is at work to accomplish our real spiritual good. We are therefore called to trust in Him, even for things that seem crooked.

Whenever we have trouble believing that God knows what He is doing, we should consider the work of our Savior. Remember that our Good Shepherd once had a crook in His lot—a crook that came in the shape of a cross. In His prayer at the Garden of Gethsemane, Jesus asked His Father if there was any way to make Calvary straight instead of crooked. But there was no other way. As Jesus considered the work of God, He could see that the only way to make atonement for our sin was to die in our place. So, Jesus suffered the crooked cross that it was his God-given lot to bear. And He trusted His Father through His sufferings, waiting for Him to straighten things out when the time was right by raising Him up on the third day.

If God can straighten out something as crooked as the cross, then surely we can trust Him to do something with the crook in our lot. This was the testimony that James Montgomery Boice gave the last time he spoke to his congregation at Philadelphia's Tenth Presbyterian Church. Dr Boice had been diagnosed with a fatal and aggressive cancer; by the time he announced his illness, he had only weeks to live. This was the crook in his lot. So, in his farewell address Dr Boice raised a serious question that was based on the sovereignty and goodness of God. 'If God does something in your life,' he asked, 'would you change it?' To say this in the way Qoheleth would have said it, 'If God put a crook in your lot, would you try to make it straight?'

Well, would you? Would you get rid of your disability or disease? Would you change your job or your financial situation? Would you change your appearance, or your abilities, or your situation in life? Or would you trust God for all the crooked things in life and wait for Him to make them straight, even if you had to wait until the resurrection, just like Jesus did when He died for you on the cross?

Dr Boice answered his rhetorical question by testifying to the goodness of God's sovereign will. He said that if we tried to change what God has done, then it wouldn't be as good; we would only make it worse.[11] The Preacher who wrote Ecclesiastes said something similar. 'Consider the work of God,' he said. 'Do not try to straighten out what God has made crooked.'

Our Savior would tell us the same thing. 'When you consider the work of God,' he would say, 'remember most of all my love for you through the crooked cross, and trust our Father to straighten everything out in His own good time.'

---

11. James Montgomery Boice, 'Final Address at Tenth Presbyterian Church', in *The Life of Dr James Montgomery Boice, 1938-2000*, edited by Philip G. Ryken (Philadelphia, PA: Tenth Presbyterian Church, 2001), 44-45.

9

DON'T FORGET!

Remember also your Creator in the days of your youth, before the evil days come and the years draw near of which you will say, 'I have no pleasure in them'.
ECCLESIASTES 12:1

According to the American Society for Aesthetic Plastic Surgery, surgeons perform more than ten million cosmetic procedures each year, almost none of them medically necessary. Journalist Beth Teitell worries about all that plastic, not so much because it is unsafe or unwise, but because all the women her age who get plastic surgery will make her look older by comparison. In a book called *Drinking Problems at the Fountain of Youth*, Teitell comments that no one is safe from this fear, not even the fabulously wealthy:

> I know women who worked hard to get into good colleges, worked their connections to land enviable jobs, married well, produced children who could pose for Ralph Lauren ads, vacation on the right islands with the right beach towels and the right heiresses—they have fractional ownerships in Cessnas, for heaven's sake—and yet if they have furrows

> and hints of upper-lip lines and puppet mouth when those around them are smoother than freshly ironed Pratesi linens, what's it all worth? In a word, nothing.[1]

Whether she knows it or not, Teitell is confronting one of the reigning idolatries of modern times: the cult of youth. For people who know they are getting older, worshiping this god or goddess demands tireless efforts to stay young. But many young people worship the same deity. Rather than respecting their elders, they look down on ideas that seem old-fashioned. They only want what is new and trendy. It is hard for them to imagine that they will ever grow old. Given the choice, some of them would rather die first.

Whether we are young or old or somewhere in between, Ecclesiastes can help us. The Preacher who wrote this book teaches us to celebrate the joys of life at any age. But he is also honest about the troubles that come with growing old. By the wisdom of the Spirit he calls us to live well, however old we happen to be.

The Joy of Youth

As sober as it is, Ecclesiastes nevertheless celebrates the strength of youth. The Solomon who wrote this book took a realistic if not pessimistic view of life's troubles. Yet even he said, 'Rejoice, O young [person], in your youth, and let your heart cheer you in the days of your youth' (Eccles. 11:9). In this way, the author charges us to *rejoice in the strength of our youth*.

Young people are truly blessed; generally speaking, they have fewer of the cares that come with having adult

---

1. Beth Teitell, *Drinking Problems at the Fountain of Youth* (William Morrow, 2008), 12-13.

responsibilities. Their bodies are strong and getting stronger. Their hearts are full of easy laughter. They have the freedom to take risks and ample time to go a new direction in life. They still dare to dream that they can make a difference in the world. And their heavenly Father confirms these blessings when He says, 'Rejoice in the strength of your youth'.

Yet even here, Ecclesiastes sounds a cautionary note. When the Preacher tells us to follow our heart, some people may be tempted to think that they can do whatever they please. This is a temptation for all of us, whether we are young or old. When we follow our hearts, it is easy to think mainly of ourselves, to expect other people to adjust to our agenda, and to take whatever we want out of life.

For some people, walking in the ways of their heart means living for the moment without stopping to think about the consequences. Rather than cleaning up after themselves, they leave a mess behind. They grab immediate pleasures without making long-term commitments. So, the Preacher makes it clear that in following our heart, we are called to holiness: 'Walk in the ways of your heart and the sight of your eyes. But know that for all these things God will bring you into judgment' (Eccles. 11:9). Then he proceeds in the next verse to warn that 'youth and the dawn of life are vanity' (Eccles. 11:10).

The Preacher knows that young people face many temptations: money, sex, image, power. He also knows that God is a righteous judge who will hold us accountable for everything we think, say, or do. So he reminds us that every time we do what looks good to us, we have to answer to God for what we have done. Young people, especially, need to beware of 'the lust of the flesh, and the lust of the eyes, and the pride of life' (1 John 2:16 KJV). The Preacher does not say this to suck the joy out of life, but to remind us that true joy flows from a heart surrendered to God.

The word 'judgment' at the end of verse 9 is literally '*the* judgment', and thus it refers to the great day when 'God judges the secrets of men by Jesus Christ' (Rom. 2:16). That day may seem as if it is too far off to make any difference in daily decision-making. But our great Judge 'looks to the ends of the earth and sees everything under the heavens' (Job 28:24). This means that everything we do matters for eternity. How we spend our money, what we do with our hands and feet, the way we use our time, what we plan for the future, how we handle our relationships—what we touch, taste, hear and see—all of this matters to God in the context of eternity.

Rejoice responsibly. Savor life's pleasures in a God-honoring way. In celebrating the gift of youth, follow God's call to 'flee youthful passions and pursue righteousness, faith, love and peace, along with those who call on the Lord from a pure heart' (2 Tim. 2:22).

The Limitations of Old Age

Here is a second charge: 'Remember also your Creator in the days of your youth' (Eccles. 12:1). As we rejoice in the strength of our youth, we must also remember our Creator-God.

To set this command in its biblical context we should fast forward to the end of life, which for most people comes in old age. In all likelihood, after a long, slow decline we will finally come to the end of our days and draw our last breath.

If it is hard for some of us to imagine what old age will be like, Ecclesiastes can help. Here the Preacher gives us one of the most memorable passages in the Bible, about the reality of our mortality. These verses also happen to comprise one of the most beautiful poems ever written about aging. The time to remember our Creator is:

> before the sun and the light and the moon and the stars are darkened and the clouds return after the rain, in the day when the keepers of the house tremble, and the strong men are bent, and the grinders cease because they are few, and those who look through the windows are dimmed, and the doors on the street are shut—when the sound of the grinding is low, and one rises up at the sound of a bird, and all the daughters of song are brought low—they are afraid also of what is high, and terrors are in the way; the almond tree blossoms, the grasshopper drags itself along, and desire fails (Eccles. 12:2-5).

On a first hearing it may be hard to appreciate what Solomon is saying, so it is important to unpack the imagery. Verse 2 compares the troubles of old age to a gathering storm. Both night and day are darkened by clouds, and after the rain falls, the storm clouds gather again. This is what happens when people grow old. When we are young, there is still time for stormy skies to clear, but old people may suffer one trouble right after another, with little or no time to recover. The light of life grows dim.

Verses 3 to 5 compare an elderly person to a house that is crumbling with decay.[2] The 'keepers of the house' are a person's arms, which start to tremble. The 'strong men' are legs bent with age. The 'grinders' are teeth, of course—if any are left. The 'windows' are eyes dimmed by cataracts or some other loss of vision. The 'doors' are ears that are deaf or hard of hearing, and thus are closed to the hum of daily life. The 'daughters of song' are vocal chords that no longer have the elastic strength to make sweet music. Since almond trees

---

2. According to an alternative interpretation, all of the images in this passage refer to a funeral procession and to the way activity ceases in a village when someone dies. See Fox, *A Time to Tear Down and a Time to Build Up*, 37.

are pale in the springtime, 'when the almond tree blossoms' refers to the season of life when a person's hair has turned white with age. Unless we happen to die young, or the world is interrupted by the Second Coming of Jesus Christ, what is described in these verses will happen to all of us: this old house will fall into ruin.

Nor are these the only debilitations that come with growing old. According to verse 4, old people have trouble sleeping; they are up with the first songbirds, rising before dawn. According to verse 5 they are afraid of falling, or else of being attacked along the road.

The elderly also suffer from diminished desire. As Pete Seeger used to sing, 'How do I know my youth is all spent? My get up and go has got up and went.' To give a biblical example, consider old Barzillai's lament when King David finally invited him to the royal palace in Jerusalem: 'I am this day eighty years old. Can I discern what is pleasant and what is not? Can your servant taste what he eats or what he drinks? Can I still listen to the voice of singing men and singing women?' (2 Sam. 19:35). In a word, the answer is 'no'.

If we fast forward to the end of life, we soon reach a scene where youthful pleasures lose their power to awaken desire. Unfortunately, when that day comes, we will no longer be able to follow the biblical exhortation to rejoice in the strength of our youth.

The Finality of Death

Even more sadly, someday the crumbling old house will collapse. The Preacher prepares us for our tragic demise with the image of the grasshopper in verse 5. Typically, grasshoppers spring up high in the air, so a grasshopper stiffly scraping itself along the ground is a goner. The same sorry fate awaits us all.

As far as Solomon is concerned, the finality of death is a good reason not to forget our Maker. Why should we remember our Creator in the days of our youth? 'Because man is going to his eternal home, and the mourners go about the streets—before the silver cord is snapped, or the golden bowl is broken, or the pitcher is shattered at the fountain, or the wheel broken at the cistern, and the dust returns to the earth as it was, and the spirit returns to God who gave it' (Eccles. 12:5b-7).

These are memorable descriptions of death. To die is to go to our eternal home. We will not live here forever. Today we are young and strong but already we are getting older, and tomorrow the mourners will carry our bodies out for burial.

Death is like the snapping of a silver cord and the shattering of a golden bowl. Something precious and beautiful is broken. To change the metaphor, death is like a wheel broken or a jar shattered at a well for drawing water. The apparatus is destroyed beyond repair, and thus it is useless for drawing life-giving water.

What else does Ecclesiastes say about death? To die is to return to the dust—the curse that God pronounced on Adam and all our sin (see Gen. 3:19). This is the same curse that Jesus suffered on the cross, for in the psalm of the God-forsaken servant, we hear Him say to His Father, 'you lay me in the dust of death' (Ps. 22:15). If it happened to Jesus, it will happen to all of us. We too are made of dust (Gen. 2:7; Ps. 103:14), and to the dust we shall return. One day, our bodies will go to the ground and our souls will return to their Maker, as death separates body from soul until the resurrection of the dead.

These are the sober realities of life and death in a fallen world—realities we all have to face, whether we are young or old.

Reasons to Remember

The reason Ecclesiastes shows us all this—the reason it confronts us with the end of life—is because what happens *then* has implications for the way we live today. The Preacher is calling us to remember our Creator *now*, before all of these bad things happen—before we get old and finally die.

The Irish rock star Bono offers an apt summary of Ecclesiastes, which happens to be one of his favorite books: 'It's a book about a character who wants to find out why he's alive, why he was created. He tries knowledge. He tries wealth. He tries experience. He tries everything. You hurry to the end of the book to find out why, and it says, "Remember your Creator." In a way, it's such a letdown. Yet it isn't.'[3]

So, remember your Creator. Grow in your relationship with the living God. Keep the God who made you clearly in mind. Know His Son. Walk with His Spirit under the lordship of Jesus Christ. This is the wise counsel of Ecclesiastes, and there are all kinds of reasons for us to follow it.

Remember your Creator because He *is* your Creator, the source of youth and strength. Today is a day to praise the God who made you. Celebrate the gifts that God has given you. Whatever capacity of reason you have, whatever skill in communication, whatever creativity in music and the arts, whatever rigor in science, whatever strength in athletics, whatever heart for friendship, whatever compassion for people in need—these are all gifts from your Creator-God. Praise Him for making you just the way you are!

Remember your Creator because He is also your Savior. Jesus Christ is the Creator-God. 'For by him all things were created, in heaven and on earth, visible and invisible, whether

---

3. Bono, quoted by Denis Haack, 'Johnny Cash: Clouded by Sin, Colored by Grace,' *byFaith* (July/August, 2005), 39.

thrones or dominions or rulers or authorities—all things were created through him and for him' (Col. 1:16). When we look at Ecclesiastes in the full scope of redemptive history, we recognize the call to remember our Creator as a call to honor Jesus Christ.

Jesus is not only our Maker, but also our Redeemer. By His death on the cross, all our sins are forgiven. So, may God have mercy on us! May the crucified Lord Jesus Christ forgive our unkind words, scornful criticisms, unclean desires, damnable curses, thoughtless lies, petty thefts, and proud idolatries. If we remember our Savior in the days of our youth, we will find mercy for all our sins.

Here is another reason to remember our Creator: the older we get, the more we forget. Eventually, we may even forget the people we love. But if we make a lifelong practice of remembering our Creator—if we maintain godly habits of daily prayer, personal Bible reading, and faithful worship and service in a local church—we will never forget the most important truths in the universe. We will always remember who our Savior is. We will know how faithfully He has walked with us all through life, and how many promises He has made to us for eternity.

Many Christians know the name of John Newton, the slave trader who came to faith in Christ and later wrote 'Amazing Grace', as well as many other compelling hymns. When Newton came to the end of his life, he famously said, 'Although my memory is fading, I remember two things very clearly: I am a great sinner and Christ is a great Savior.' If we remember our Creator-Savior in the days of our youth, then we will never forget these truths—not even on the day of death.

Here is another reason to remember our Creator in the days of our youth: if we remember Him now, we will be able to dedicate the rest of our lives to His service. So, remember

Jesus while you still have your wits about you. Remember Him while you are charting His course for your life. Remember Him before you make a lot of bad decisions you will later regret. Remember Him now, while you still have the rest of your life to give for His glory. 'Many have remembered too late,' wrote Charles Bridges, but 'none too soon.'[4]

One account of Billy Graham's famous crusades at Madison Square Garden tells the story of an old man who was watching a television broadcast back home in North Carolina. The man had attended church all his life, but he had never made a personal commitment to Jesus Christ. Although his minister had often pressed him to make a spiritual decision, he had always resisted.

Yet, as Billy Graham went off the air that night, the man began to sob heavily in his chair. When his wife asked him what was wrong, he said, 'I have given my heart to Christ. I have finally given my heart to Christ.'

When the woman awoke the next morning, she was surprised to see that her husband was not in bed. She found him outside in the flower garden, lying face down on the ground, dead of a heart attack.[5]

The story of the man from North Carolina is a story of God's grace. Where there is life, there is hope. It is never too late for any living person to trust in Jesus for salvation. But the story is also a tragedy, because if that old man had remembered his Creator in the days of his youth, he could have offered a whole life of service to Jesus, not just his last day. None of us ever knows how long we have left to live. But one thing we know: it is never too soon to start living for Jesus.

---

4. Bridges, *Commentary on Ecclesiastes*, 294.

5. Curtis Mitchell, *God in the Garden: The Story of the Billy Graham New York Crusade* (Garden City, NY: Doubleday, 1957), 16.

In my work as President of Wheaton College, I was deeply touched to receive a bequest from the estate of Shannon Wilkes, a recent alumna. As a campus community, we had often prayed for Shannon in our chapel services. She matriculated at Wheaton to play soccer as well as to study, and she played for a team that won the NCAA Championship. The following year she was diagnosed with cancer, and after a five-year struggle, she went home to be with her Savior.

Shannon Wilkes was known for her humility, courage, perseverance and selfless love. She did not allow intense physical suffering to diminish her trust in her Savior. Nor did she let it prevent her from earning her college degree: despite her prognosis, she was preparing to spend a lifetime serving Christ and His Kingdom. Shannon's final act of stewardship was to give whatever remained of her financial resources to Wheaton College—a precious gift to help other students receive a Christ-centered education. In short, Shannon Wilkes remembered her Creator in the days of her youth.

The Best Reason of All

There are many good reasons to remember God. But here is the best reason of all: remember your Creator because He remembers you.

The God who made you rejoices that He made you just the way you are. He celebrates the gifts that He has given you, the way those gifts have developed, and the purpose He has for you in life.

Your Savior remembers who you are. He has been thinking about you since eternity past. He had you in mind when He went to the cross, when He came up from the grave, and when He ascended to glory. He has been watching over you every day of your life. Furthermore, He has promised to remember you when He comes into his kingdom. He will not lose track of you, but raise you up to everlasting life.

This promise of God's remembrance was of special comfort during the last years of my grandfather's life, when the old man had Alzheimer's. By the time he was in his early nineties, my grandfather found it hard to remember much of anything (including, on occasion, who he was). This was extremely distressing for him—he knew that he was confused, but he didn't know why. 'I can't remember who I am!' he said to my mother.

'That's okay, Dad,' she replied, 'I know who you are, and I can take care of everything you need.'

God has an excellent memory. He will not forget us. And because of this, on the last of all days our bodies will be fully restored. Everything that crumbled and decayed will be made new. In effect, our old house will become a new house: 'For we know that if the tent that is our earthly home is destroyed, we have a building from God, a house not made with hands, eternal in the heavens' (2 Cor. 5:1). All of which is more than enough reason to remember your Creator-God and risen Savior, Jesus Christ.

10

THE FINAL ANALYSIS

The end of the matter; all has been heard. Fear God and keep his commandments, for this is the whole duty of man. For God will bring every deed into judgment, with every secret thing, whether good or evil.

Ecclesiastes 12:13-14

If there is no God, then there is no Judge. If there is no Judge, then there will be no Final Judgment. If there is no Final Judgment, there is no ultimate meaning to life.

This is the logic of Quentin's argument in *After the Fall* by Arthur Miller. Quentin says:

> For many years I looked at life like a case at law. It was a series of proofs. When you're young you prove how brave you are, or smart; then, what a good lover; then, a good father; finally, how wise, or powerful… . But underlying it all, I see now, there was a presumption. That one moved … on an upward path toward some elevation, where … God knows what … I would be justified, or even condemned. A verdict anyway. I think now that my disaster really began

> when I looked up one day … and the bench was empty. No judge in sight. And all that remained was the endless argument with oneself, this pointless litigation of existence before an empty bench.… Which, of course, is another way of saying—despair.[1]

By Quentin's logic, if there is no God to judge the world, then human existence is a pointless litigation that ends in meaningless despair. The Solomon who wrote Ecclesiastes would have agreed. From the beginning of his book he has been saying that if there is no God, there is no meaning.

What He Said

'Vanity of vanities … all is vanity' (Eccles. 12:8). These were the Preacher's first (see Eccles. 1:2) and also his last words—a literary technique known as *inclusio*. The writer begins and ends his composition by saying the same thing.

Throughout Ecclesiastes, the Hebrew word for vanity (*hevel*) has served as the Preacher's multipurpose metaphor to express the futility of life in a fallen world. Taken literally, the word refers to a breath or vapor, like the steam rising from a warm lake on a chilly morning. Such is life: it vanishes into thin air. Everything is ephemeral.[2]

The vapor of our existence is dramatized in *Breath*, a play by Samuel Beckett that lasts a mere thirty-five seconds. As the curtain opens, there is a pile of rubbish on the stage, illuminated by a single light. The light dims and then brightens a little before going completely out. There are no

1. Arthur Miller, *After the Fall* (1964), quoted in Keller, *Reason for God*, 156, 57.
2. I am borrowing this turn of phrase from Richard Schultz, 'Ecclesiastes,' 605.

words or actors in the drama, only a sound track with the cry of a human voice, followed by an inhaled breath, an exhaled breath, and another cry. The short play depicts what David wrote in one of his psalms: 'mankind is a mere breath' (Ps. 39:11; cf. 39:5).

By beginning and ending with the same statement about life's vanity, the structure of Ecclesiastes reinforces the point that there is 'nothing new under the sun' (Eccles. 1:9). As it was before, so it is now, and so it will ever be. All is vanity, all the time. We end up right back where we began.

We should not think, however, that the Preacher merely repeats himself. Ecclesiastes 12:8 brings us back to the place where we began, but we are not the same people that we were when we first started reading the book. Studying Ecclesiastes has given us a bigger perspective on life. So, when we hear the same statement at the end that we heard at the beginning, it strikes us with greater force.

Now we know that work is vanity; there is nothing for us to gain from all our restless toil under the sun (e.g. Eccles. 1:3). We also know that merely human wisdom is vanity, because whether we are wise or foolish, we will all die in the end (Eccles. 2:15-16). We know as well that pleasure is vanity. Wine, women and song; houses and vineyards; gold and silver—there is 'nothing to be gained under the sun' (Eccles. 2:11).

It is all vanity. Power is vanity: there is no one to comfort the tears of the oppressed (Eccles. 4:1). Money is vanity, too, because it cannot satisfy our souls (Eccles. 5:10). Then there is the last of all vanities, which is returning to the earth from which we were made. Dust we are, and to the dust we shall return (Eccles. 3:20).

Not that we never have *any* joy, of course. Qoheleth has told us to eat and drink and find satisfaction in our work (e.g.

Eccles. 2:24). There is a time for healing and harvesting, a time for laughing and dancing (Eccles. 3:1-8). Rejoice in the prosperity that God so richly provides (Eccles. 5:19; 7:14), the Preacher says; enjoy life with the one you love (Eccles. 9:9). There is joy in the world under the blessing of a faithful God.

Ecclesiastes mainly teaches us to see how meaningless life is without God, and how little joy there is under the sun if we try to leave our Creator out of His universe. By the time we get to the end of the book, we have to admit that the author has proved his case. 'Nothing in our search has led us home,' writes Derek Kidner; 'nothing that we are offered under the sun is ours to keep.'[3] Vanity of vanities! It is all vanity.

How He said it

Yet 'vanity' does not get the last word, either in the Bible or in the Christian life. Ecclesiastes might well have ended with chapter 12, verse 8: 'Vanity of vanities!' Instead, it closes with further remarks that put the whole book into perspective.

The epilogue to Ecclesiastes may have been written by someone else. There is some 'authorial ambiguity' here.[4] Clearly the Preacher is still speaking in verse 8, but when we get to verse 9 there is a shift. Someone refers to the original author in the third person, as if to say: 'Now let me give you my own perspective on all this.'[5] Some scholars even think that there are two epilogues, one in verses 9 to 11 from someone who agrees with the Preacher, and one in verses 12 to 14 from someone who tries to correct him.[6]

---

3. Kidner, *Message of Ecclesiastes*, 104.

4. Treier, *Proverbs & Ecclesiastes*, 227.

5. Iain Provan, *Ecclesiastes/Song of Songs*, NIV Application Commentary (Grand Rapids, MI: Zondervan, 2001), 226.

6. Whybray, *Ecclesiastes*, 169.

But what purpose would an editor have in publishing a book with which he disagreed almost entirely?

Possibly the last six verses were written by someone other than Qoheleth, the Preacher-King. But when we look carefully, we find the epilogue affirming both what the author said and the way that he said it, before finally applying his teaching in a practical way to our life before God. The book's closing words are a proper conclusion rather than a possible contradiction to everything that has come before. So there is little if any need to speculate about multiple authors.

Up until now, Ecclesiastes has told us *what* the Preacher said. Now the book tells us *how* he said it: 'Besides being wise, the Preacher also taught the people knowledge, weighing and studying and arranging many proverbs with great care. The Preacher sought to find words of delight, and uprightly he wrote words of truth' (Eccles. 12:9-10).

The Preacher wrote with *logical clarity*. He took the time and trouble to evaluate all the wise sayings that he had heard, and then he included the ones that were weighty enough to demand our full attention—proverbs such as 'who can make straight what [God] has made crooked?' (Eccles. 7:13). If the Preacher was actually King Solomon, as many people think, then what Ecclesiastes says about studying proverbs would make sense: King Solomon heard many wise sayings over the course of his lifetime (according to 1 Kings 4:32 he was able to quote three thousand proverbs), but he included in the Bible only the ones that were wise and true.

Not only did the Preacher assess these proverbs studiously, he also arranged them carefully. Contrary to the complaints of scholars who say that there is 'no progression of thought from one section to another' and that the author 'offers no universal or satisfactory answer' to any of the problems he raises, there is sufficient logic in the way this book is put together.[7] Ecclesiastes is constructed as a complete work of literature, in which the author states his theme (Eccles. 1:1-11), tells us the story of his quest to find meaning in life (Eccles. 1:12-6:12), shows us the difference between wisdom and folly (Eccles. 7-11), and then closes by talking about death and dying (Eccles. 12:1-7) before restating his primary theme: the vanity of all vanity (Eccles. 12:8).

Even the sections of Ecclesiastes that seem to meander serve the book's logical aims. Dan Treier argues that 'the book's form fits its meaning' and wonders

> if Ecclesiastes actually mirrors the Sage's life narrative—beginning with a quest in clearly delimited stages; eventually turning to repeated musings on key themes along with aphoristic wisdom as the best available possibilities; and continually raising the stakes, regarding God and death, joy and knowledge, until concluding with the most intense yet elusive material....Ecclesiastes does not proceed via linear argument the way modern Westerners might expect or impose as interpreters, themes and motifs have accumulating effects as they recur....The overall effect is a looping or lumbering one, in which the text steps forward to explore territory before doubling back to take another path, only to revisit earlier areas from new angles.[8]

In addition to writing with logical clarity, the Preacher also wrote with *literary artistry*. He sought to find 'words of delight' (Eccles. 12:10)—a marvelous phrase that expresses

---

7. R. Norman Whybray, *Ecclesiastes*, Old Testament Guides (Edinburgh: T & T Clark, 1989), 17.

8. Treier, *Proverbs & Ecclesiastes*, 133-134.

the beauty of the Bible. Whether people agree with the Preacher's theology or not, no one criticizes his writing style. The American writer Tom Wolfe described Ecclesiastes as 'the highest flower of poetry, eloquence, and truth'—'the greatest single piece of writing I have known.'[9] This is the book that gave us phrases such as 'the sun also rises' (Eccles. 1:5), 'to everything a season' (Eccles. 3:1), 'eternity in the hearts of men' (Eccles. 3:11), 'when the almond tree blossoms' (Eccles. 12:5) and 'man knows not his time' (Eccles. 9:12). Praise God for the beauty of Ecclesiastes—not just what the book says, but also the way the book says it. Here, as everywhere, the Word of God pleases the ear, inspires the imagination, and fascinates the mind.

The Preacher also wrote with *intellectual integrity*. Once he had found words of delight, he 'uprightly wrote words of truth' (Eccles. 12:10). He wrote truthfully as well as stylishly. If there is one thing we can always count on Qoheleth to do, it is to tell us the truth about God and about life in a fallen world. *Moby Dick* thus describes Ecclesiastes as 'a fine-hammered steel of woe.'[10] Whether he is talking about the agonies of old age, or the anguish of losing a fortune, the Preacher never holds back from telling us what life is really like under the sun.

Why He Said It

The author of Ecclesiastes wrote with clarity, artistry, and integrity. But before we leave this book behind, we still need to ask 'Why? What was the Preacher's reason for telling us about life's vanity?'

9. Tom Wolfe, quoted in Robert Short, *A Time to Be Born—A Time to Die* (New York: Harper and Row, 1973), ix.

10. Herman Melville, *Moby Dick*, quoted in Johnston, *Useless Beauty*, 20.

Ecclesiastes closes with a clear purpose statement: 'The words of the wise are like goads, and like nails firmly fixed are the collected sayings; they are given by one Shepherd' (Eccles. 12:11).

A 'goad' is one of the tools of a shepherd's trade, a sharp stick that spurs a stubborn beast to keep moving. Ecclesiastes does the same thing for people of faith. It is like the books that Franz Kafka wanted to read—'books that wound and stab us,' or that serve as 'the axe for the frozen sea inside us.'[11]

Think of Ecclesiastes as the Bible's cattle prod. The Preacher's words push us to expect lasting satisfaction not in money or pleasure, but only in the goodness of God. They steer us away from foolish rage and mocking laughter. They spur us on to patience, contentment, and joy. When we forget about God the Preacher prompts us to remember our Creator, and the moment we start to think that we will live forever, he pokes us in the ribs and reminds us that soon we will die.

Ecclesiastes also compares the Preacher's words to 'nails firmly fixed.' This is not a prophecy of the crucifixion, as some have thought, but an image of permanence and fixity. Once a wise saying is driven into the mind it stays there, like a nail pounded into a block of wood.

The biblical proverbs have a way of nailing us right in the conscience. They also have a way of sticking in our brains. Once we hear them, we never forget them. There are many such proverbs in Ecclesiastes: 'a threefold cord is not quickly broken' (Eccles. 4:9, 12); 'the race is not to the swift, nor the battle to the strong … but time and chance happen to them all' (Eccles. 9:11); and so forth.

---

11. Franz Kafka, quoted in E. G. Singgih, 'An Axe for the Frozen Sea: The Emerging Task of Theological Education and the Role of the Librarians,' *Asia Journal of Theology* 12 (1998), 202-3.

All of these words—the wise sayings that get nailed into our hearts and that goad us into action—are 'given by one Shepherd' (Eccles. 12:11). Possibly this refers to the Preacher himself, since he has identified himself as 'king over Israel in Jerusalem' (see Eccles. 1:12). In the ancient world, kings were often considered to be the shepherds of their people. So it would make sense for the Solomon of Ecclesiastes to identify himself as a shepherd as well as a preacher.

More likely, though, the 'shepherd' is God Himself (which is why the term is capitalized in some translations). The act of giving wisdom helps us to see the connection: the Shepherd who 'gives' wise words in Ecclesiastes 12:11 is the same God who 'gives' wisdom and knowledge in Ecclesiastes 2:26. Chapter 12 marks the first time that the title 'Shepherd' has appeared in Ecclesiastes, which seems to distinguish the Shepherd from the Preacher, rather than to identify the two.[12] Furthermore, 'Shepherd' is one of the noble titles for God in the Old Testament, not only in Psalm 23, but also in places such as Psalm 80, where He is called the 'Shepherd of Israel' (Ps. 80:1; cf. 78:72). Even more significantly, the prophet Ezekiel uses the expression 'one shepherd' to refer to the Messiah, the Son of David (see Ezek. 34:23, 37:24). All things considered, it is best to recognize the 'one Shepherd' in Ecclesiastes 12 as the one and only Shepherd: God Almighty.

Seeing the author of Ecclesiastes as our divine shepherd helps us remember that his words are not merely the musings of some skeptical philosopher; they are part of the inspired, infallible, and inerrant revelation of Almighty God. As the Shepherd of our souls, God uses this book to prod us into spiritual action.

---

12. Eaton, *Ecclesiastes*, 154.

This claim has even greater force when we remember that our Shepherd has become our Savior. If Jesus Christ is the Good Shepherd who lays down His life for His sheep (John 10:11)—the person whom the Gospels identify as the 'one shepherd' for the flock of God (John 10:16)—then the words we read in Ecclesiastes are also His words. Jesus is the one calling us away from the vanity of life without God to find joy and meaning in His grace. He wants us to know that we are not just living 'under the sun'. We are living under the Son—the Son of God who 'loved us and gave himself up for us' (Eph. 5:2).

Books without End

To read Ecclesiastes is to hear our Shepherd's voice, including this final warning: 'My son, beware of anything beyond these. Of making many books there is no end, and much study is a weariness of the flesh' (Eccles. 12:12).

What Ecclesiastes says about writing and reading can be confirmed by every scholar who has ever lived. Already in the ancient world, royal libraries were full of books. In response to contemporaries who spent a fortune amassing large personal libraries, the Stoic philosopher and statesman Seneca observed that 'the abundance of books is distraction'.[13] Similarly, the German philosopher and mathematician Gottfried Wilhelm Leibniz complained that the 'horrible mass of books' being published in the late seventeenth century threatened to consign every author to 'the danger of general oblivion.'[14]

13. Seneca, quoted in Ann M. Blair, *Too Much to Know: Managing Scholarly Information before the Information Age* (New Haven, CT: Yale University Press, 2011), 15.

14. Gottfried Wilhelm Leibniz, quoted in Blair, *Too Much to Know*, 58.

What would Leibniz say today, when more than a million new books are published every year?[15] Add to these titles the astonishing growth of digital information. As of April 15, 2014, a Google search for the term 'information overload' yielded more than 16 million hits. So, what the Bible says is true: of the making of many books there is no end, and studying even some of them is enough to wear anyone out.

Of course there is a place in Christian discipleship for the life of the mind. But we should always remember that human wisdom is extremely limited. How many books have been written! Yet how little most of them teach us about the knowledge of God! By far the most important book for us to study is the Bible, including everything in Ecclesiastes.

In *The Great Divorce*, C. S. Lewis describes a man from the suburbs of hell who has spent his whole life seeking the truth, or so he says. The man wanders near the borders of heaven, where, by the gracious invitation of God, he is invited to enter. But the Spirit warns him: 'I can promise you … no atmosphere of inquiry, for I will bring you to the land not of questions but of answers, and you shall see the face of God.'

The man is not quite ready to let go of his quest, however. He wants to study some more before he accepts anyone else's conclusions. So he says, 'We must all interpret those beautiful words in our own way! For me there is no such thing as a final answer. The free wind of inquiry must *always* continue to blow through the mind, must it not?'

'Listen!' God's Spirit says to the man: 'Once you were a child. Once you knew what inquiry was for. There was a

15. The United Nations Educational, Scientific and Cultural Organization (UNESCO) publishes these statistics annually.

time when you asked questions because you wanted answers, and were glad when you had found them. Become that child again: even now.'

Sadly, the man refuses. 'When I became a man,' he says, 'I put away childish things.' The conversation suddenly ends when he remembers that he has an appointment, makes his apologies, and hurries off to join a discussion group in hell.[16]

Are you still seeking for spiritual truth? End that quest and surrender to the God of all knowledge. Trust Jesus even before you have all the answers. Do not be like the person Paul warned Timothy about: 'always learning and never able to arrive at a knowledge of the truth' (2 Tim. 3:7). Be content with what the Bible says, not accepting anything less, and not demanding anything more (cf. Rev. 22:18-19).

All There Is

We have heard what the Preacher said, as well as how and why he said it. So how should we respond? How does the book end?

The last words of Ecclesiastes provide both an ethical and an eschatological conclusion: 'The end of the matter; all has been heard. Fear God and keep his commandments, for this is the whole duty of man. For God will bring every deed into judgment, with every secret thing, whether good or evil' (Eccles. 12:13-14).

To fear God is to honor and revere Him as God. This is not the first time that Ecclesiastes has told us to do this. The Preacher has told us to fear God because He demands holy worship (Eccles. 5:7). He has said that we should fear God in times of adversity as well as prosperity (Eccles. 7:14-18). If we do fear God, he said, it will go well with us (Eccles. 8:12).

---

16. C. S. Lewis, *The Great Divorce* (London: Geoffrey Bles 1945), 40ff.

Here is how Michael Eaton summarizes Qoheleth's perspective on the fear of God:

> It is not only the beginning of wisdom; it is also the beginning of joy, of contentment and of an energetic and purposeful life. The Preacher wishes to deliver us from a rosy-colored, self-confident, godless life, with its inevitable cynicism and bitterness, and from trusting in wisdom, pleasure, wealth and human justice or integrity. He wishes to drive us to see that God is there, that He is good and generous, and that only such an outlook makes life coherent and fulfilling.[17]

At the end of Ecclesiastes we are told to fear God because one day we will fall into His hands for judgment. Whether we are ready to come before God now, or hope to avoid Him, the truth is that one day every one of us will stand before God for judgment. One day God will expose every secret sin and uncover every anonymous kindness. He will bring every last deed to judgment, whether it is good or evil, including every casual thought and every careless word (see Matt. 12:36). He 'will bring to light the things now hidden in darkness and will disclose the purposes of the heart' (1 Cor. 4:5).

Ecclesiastes has told us this before. After all our days of questing, when we reach the end of our spiritual road, we will arrive at the throne of eternal justice and meet the Great Judge. Qoheleth says this again here at the end because it means that in the final analysis, everything matters.

The Preacher began and ended his spiritual quest by saying that everything is vanity, that without God there is no meaning or purpose to life. 'Is that all there is?' he kept

---

17. Eaton, *Ecclesiastes*, 48.

asking. 'Isn't there more to life than what I see under the sun?' If there is no God, and therefore no final judgment, then it is hard to see how anything we do really matters. But if there is a God who will judge the world, then *everything* matters. This is *not* all there is. There is a God in heaven who rules the world. There is a life to come. One day the dead will be raised and every person who has ever lived will stand before God. And when that day comes, it will become clear that there is eternal significance in everything that anyone ever thought, said or did.

It will matter how we used our time, whether we wasted it on foolish pleasures or worked hard for the Lord. It will matter what we did with our money, whether we spent it on ourselves or invested it in the eternal kingdom. It will matter what we did with our bodies—what our eyes saw, our hands touched and our mouths spoke. What we did for a two-year-old will matter—the way we made time for her and got down on her level. What we said about someone else's performance will matter—the sarcastic comment or the word of genuine praise. The proud boast and the selfless sacrifice will matter. The household task and the homework assignment will matter. The cup of water, the tear of compassion, the word of testimony—all of it will matter.

The final message of Ecclesiastes is not that nothing matters, therefore, but that *everything* does. What we did, how we did it, and why we did it will all have eternal significance. Everything in the universe is subject to the final verdict of a righteous God who knows every secret. The things we do (and do not do) *today* will all be seen in the light of the final judgment.

If this is true, then what matters the most is the personal decision that each person makes about Jesus Christ. Ecclesiastes ends with a warning of judgment, not a promise of grace. But this warning still points us to the gospel. If God will bring everything to judgment, then it is desperately important to make sure that we will be justified on that great day. The only way to be sure is to entrust our lives to Jesus Christ, who alone has the mercy to save us from the justice of God.

Our Savior fully entered into the vanity of this fallen world. Like us, He suffered its futility and frustration. But Jesus did more. He took the judgment that we deserve by dying for our sins on the cross. Then His body was laid in the dust, like the Preacher said. But He rose again miraculously on the third day, bringing life out of the grave.

Soon our Savior will come again, on the day when 'God judges the secrets of men by Christ Jesus' (Rom. 2:16). The Bible says that God 'has fixed a day on which he will judge the world in righteousness by a man whom he has appointed; and of this he has given assurance to all by raising him from the dead' (Acts 17:31).

The Bible also says that when the great day comes, people who trust in Jesus will not 'come into judgment' but will pass 'from death to life' (John 5:24). By faith, we will stand before our righteous Judge and fall into the arms of a loving Savior. The victory of Jesus will save us from the vanity of sin.

ISBN 978-1-78191-307-9

Salvation by Crucifixion

Philip G. Ryken

Ryken celebrates Easter with this thoughtful guidebook to understanding the cross. Seven answers to seven questions explain the why and the wherefore of the cross for a Biblical faith and a Christian life.

Read this book slowly, prayerfully, meditatively, and let its amazing truths penetrate the depth of your soul.

Joel R. Beeke,
President, Puritan Reformed Theological Seminary, Grand Rapids, Michigan

The cross is the center of the Christian life and message... But what does it mean? And how does that apply to our lives? This little book will help explain that to interested readers.

Josh Moody,
Senior Pastor, College Church, Wheaton, Illinois

Perfect for a thoughtful person who wants to know Christ and discover what it means to trust in Him.

Colin S. Smith,
Senior Pastor, The Orchard, Arlington Heights, Illinois and
President, Unlocking the Bible

Artful, but simple; compact, but loaded; sound, but fresh. This book is a jewel. Some passages sing. It well repays the time it takes to read it.

Mark Dever,
Senior Pastor, Capitol Hill Baptist Church and
President, 9Marks.org, Washington, DC

Dr. Ryken in his striking exploration of this question shows the many facets of the Bible's teaching on the cross. Jesus' identity and mission shine out clearly. This book will be interesting and helpful for Christians and non-Christians alike.

W. Robert Godfrey,
President, Westminster Seminary in California, Escondido, California

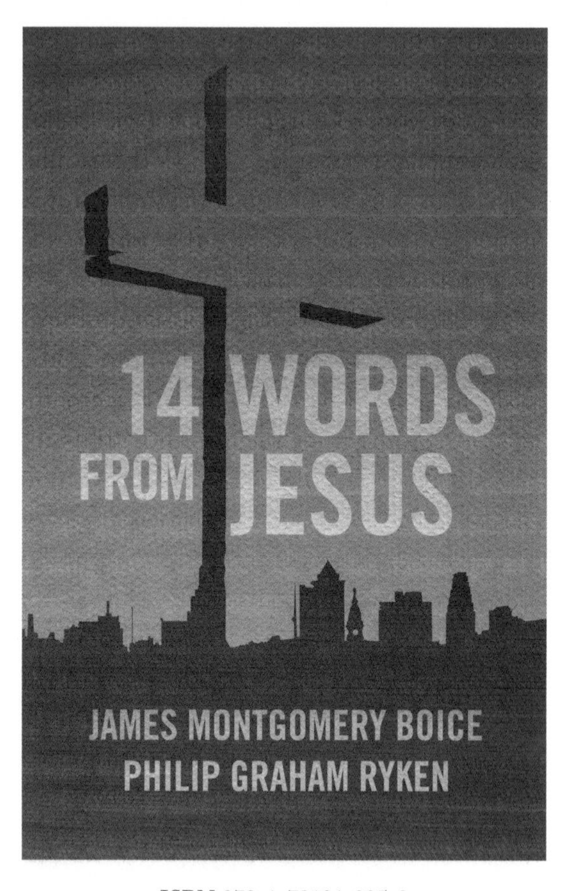

ISBN 978-1-78191-205-8

14 Words from Jesus

James Montgomery Boice & Philip G. Ryken

These inspirational readings probe Christ's seven words from the cross and equally significant, seven words from the risen Lord, after his death. These words highlight the glory of Calvary, the heart of God and how wonderfully Jesus understood that his death and resurrection was to be effective in bringing into being atonement from sin for those seeking forgiveness.

> Boice and Ryken are both excellent preachers, but first and foremost they are writing as men who have themselves been transformed by the words of Jesus. Reading this book, his words will come to you freshly too and you cannot help but marvel at his saving and transforming work.
>
> Adrian Reynolds,
> Director of Ministry, The Proclamation Trust

> ... a valuable gift to a Christian friend, and might well be read in a devotional manner with great enjoyment and benefit.
>
> Evangelicals Now

> It is a delight to me personally and a privilege for the Christian world generally to have these examples of their Biblical ministry made available by Christian Focus.
>
> Eric Alexander,
> formerly minister of St George's Tron, Glasgow

ISBN 978-1-78191-062-7

Coping With Change - Ecclesiastes

Walter C. Kaiser Jr.

Ecclesiastes is a book filled with good news for those struggling to make sense of what is happening in life. Why does man madly pursue one thing and then another without meaning? True joy comes from the Lord himself, and for the one who has learned to fear God and keep his commandments, all of life holds purpose and delight. In *Coping with Change*, noted theologian Walter Kaiser mines the riches of Ecclesiastes to reveal the source of true joy.

Perhaps the most helpful feature of Kaiser's treatment is that he believes the book has a discernible plan and a traceable argument and that Qoheleth was not a cynical old goat who drank Drano or vinegar for breakfast. That makes a difference in the way you understand Ecclesiastes. Buy your own copy and find out how.

Dale Ralph Davis,
Minister in Residence, First Presbyterian Church, Columbia, South Carolina

Ecclesiastes is a wisdom writing from ancient Israel but there is no book more relevant for our postmodern world today. Dr. Walter Kaiser, one of our best biblical scholars, has given us a lively commentary on this part of God's Word, one that will help us face today's changing world with integrity and faithfulness.

Timothy George,
Founding Dean of Beeson Divinity School,
Samford University, Birmingham, Alabama

Walt Kaiser's *Coping with Change* walks us through the book of Ecclesiastes, functioning like a scholarly tour guide through the mind of a man who had seen and done and achieved it all--and has realized that everything is a "mist" without God

Owen Strachan,
Associate Professor of Christian Theology,
Midwestern Baptist Theological Seminary, Kansas City, Missouri

ISBN 978-1-857952-095-6

Sure I Believe – So What?

James Montgomery Boice

No matter how enthusiastically we embrace doctrinal teaching it has no real power unless accompanied by action. James Boice tackles key areas of conflict in the Christian's life – avoiding hypocrisy, guarding our tongues using our wealth appropriately, perseverance.

If you really believe then it will show in your life. James is a practical book, too practical in dealing with our own shortcomings, errors and sins! And it is so direct that we cannot easily dismiss or escape from James' teaching. Prepare to be challenged!

> "This exposition of James is one of Boice's most practical books and has abiding relevance for Christian men and women today. Readers will gain a richer understanding of what it means to have a faith that really works."

Philip G. Ryken,
President, Wheaton College, Wheaton, Illinois

> 'James Boice was one of the greatest Bible teachers of the twentieth century. This exposition of James is an outstanding help, displaying Boice's penetrating mind and easy to read style. I warmly commend it to pastors and all other Bible students.'

Eric Alexander,
formerly minister of St George's Tron, Glasgow

Christian Focus Publications

Our mission statement –

STAYING FAITHFUL

In dependence upon God we seek to impact the world through literature faithful to His infallible Word, the Bible. Our aim is to ensure that the Lord Jesus Christ is presented as the only hope to obtain forgiveness of sin, live a useful life and look forward to heaven with Him.

Our books are published in four imprints:

CHRISTIAN FOCUS

Popular works including biographies, commentaries, basic doctrine and Christian living.

CHRISTIAN HERITAGE

Books representing some of the best material from the rich heritage of the church.

MENTOR

Books written at a level suitable for Bible College and seminary students, pastors, and other serious readers. The imprint includes commentaries, doctrinal studies, examination of current issues and church history.

CF4•K

Children's books for quality Bible teaching and for all age groups: Sunday school curriculum, puzzle and activity books; personal and family devotional titles, biographies and inspirational stories – because you are never too young to know Jesus!

Christian Focus Publications Ltd,
Geanies House, Fearn, Ross-shire,
IV20 1TW, Scotland, United Kingdom.
www.christianfocus.com